FARMSTEADS

of the California Coast

by Sarah Henry

photography by Erin Scott

yellow pear press

FARMSTEADS

of the California Coast

Photo previous page: Green String farmers, Quanah Hale, James Williams and Matty Fishkin till the field.

ISBN: 978-0-9905370-7-6

Library of Congress Cataloging-in-Publication data available upon request.
Manufactured in Hong Kong.

Design by Rose Wright.
This book has been set in Myriad Pro.

10 9 8 7 6 5 4 3 2 1

Yellow Pear Press, LLC.
www.yellowpearpress.com
Distributed by Publisher's Group West

TABLE OF CONTENTS

Farm country
calms the mind,
reinvigorates the body,
and feeds the soul.

INTRODUCTION

Farming on the Edge

It takes talent and tenacity to raise nourishing food to feed hungry people well.

The farming professionals who do the hard, dirty work of cultivating the pristine produce, delicious dairy, and sumptuous shellfish that we devour deserve celebration and are worthy of our respect, gratitude, and admiration.

That's the premise behind *Farmsteads of the California Coast.* Meet a dozen standout growers who shine on the edge of the Golden State. There's an embarrassment of riches to choose from: Whittling down the list of candidates proved tough; so many farmers, makers, and producers merit our appreciation and attention here.

Photographer Erin Scott and I selected farmsteads that represent the best of this resource-rich region and showcase its product diversity: from apple and grape growers in the north to citrus and avocado farmers in the south. Each farmer reflects a unique point of view. Some, such as Bob Cannard of Green String Farm in Petaluma, have toiled in the soil for decades and are legends in the field of alternative agriculture. Others, like Andrew Zlot of Double 8 Dairy, also in Petaluma, are career changers, trying their

hand at a back-to-the-land lifestyle and farming for the first time. In Zlot's case, with a novel, niche product: water buffalo gelato.

In these pages we share the stories and images of the quirky edible entrepreneurs on the progressive West Coast who grow our food with care, compassion, and commitment. Find oystermen and greens growers, dairy farmers, winemakers, coffee producers, and, it's true, the odd water buffalo rancher in the mix.

A farmstead includes agricultural land, along with barns, farmstands, and other structures contained on a property. Farmsteads are also places where food producers make and sell value-added products like pickles and preserves, or wine and cheese, handcrafted in small batches using raw ingredients sourced on site. There's an emphasis on

making sustainable goods that serve people *and* the planet. And, of course, they must taste terrific.

Farmsteads also evoke a state of well being. Nature nudges us to acknowledge its presence, from the sight of wide, open spaces and flourishing field crops to happy, gamboling goats. You're immersed in the rich, earthy aroma of healthy soil and the fragrant perfume of beneficial wildflowers. You hear the steady buzz of honey bees and the random vocalizations of farm animals. You feel the sting of the wind on your face, the heat of the sun on your back, and the delicious grit of dirt under your nails. At its best, farm country calms the mind, reinvigorates the body, and feeds the soul.

The farmsteads in this book have larger goals beyond meeting the needs of their

local community and customers, though they do these things, too, in all their rustic glory. These food movement mavericks' farms serve as social hubs, education centers, and locations for exploring social justice, political, and environmental matters.

Small family farms continue to thrive on the California coast, despite economic and social challenges to a way of life that was once commonplace. At Navarro Vineyards and The Apple Farm, both in Philo, Hog Island Oyster Company in Marshall, and Point Reyes Farmstead Cheese, generations of farmers work side-by-side. Farmers who grew up in the fields, such as Mickey Murch at Gospel Flat Farm in Bolinas, and Robert Abbott at Hilltop & Canyon Farms in Carpinteria, have returned home to raise their own families. It's a rural idyll that makes sense the minute you step foot on a farm and spot a young child contentedly sitting in the dirt chewing on a weed while watching mom or dad work.

Other farmers have systematically and thoughtfully restored neglected properties and nurtured and coaxed back abused land, turning them into successful independent businesses in the process. One example among many here is Dee Harley of Harley Farms Goat Dairy in picturesque Pescadero.

All these farms are known for innovation. Jim Cochran at Swanton Berry Farm, also in Pescadero, is a leader in farm worker advocacy. At neighboring Pie Ranch, farm couple Nancy Vail and Jered Lawson explore food justice concerns through hands-on education. These growers have also garnered well-deserved reputations for specialty crops. Consider Jay Ruskey of Good Land Organics in Goleta, who keeps the naysayers at bay by producing coffee beans—yes, coffee beans—in temperate California, no less.

This book is a salute to the pioneering farmers of a region blessed with incredible natural resources. Read on to discover more about the people and places whose charming and eclectic farmsteads dot this stunning coastline and reflect their owners' unique personalities and perspectives. If learning more entices you to take your own field trip to get to know your farmer and your food, then our work here is complete.

And when you dig into those briny bivalves, crunchy greens, crisp apples, sweet, juicy strawberries, creamy gelato, and bitter coffee, take a moment to give thanks to the farmstead workers who make this scrumptious California coastal feast possible.

Sarah Henry

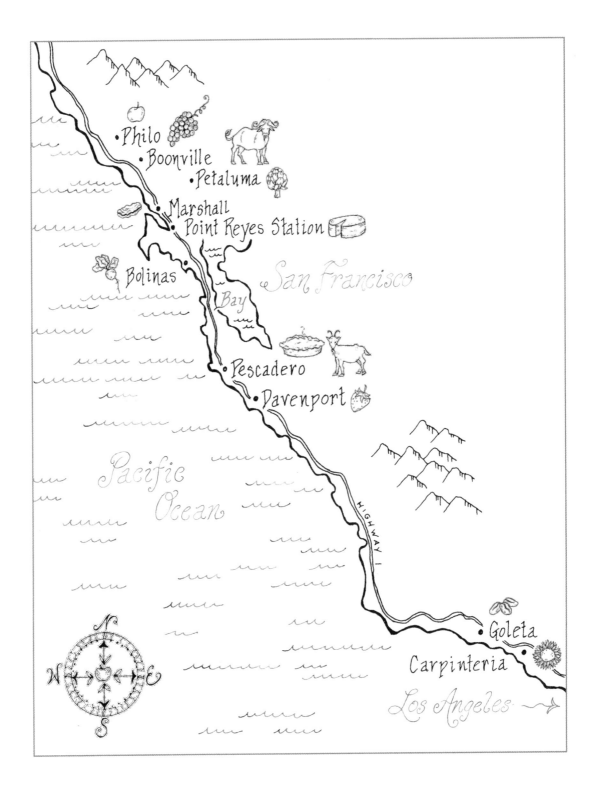

- Philo
- Boonville
- Petaluma
- Marshall
- Point Reyes Station
- Bolinas
- Pescadero
- Davenport

San Francisco

Bay

Pacific Ocean

HIGHWAY 1

- Goleta

Carpinteria

Los Angeles →

N
W E
S

FARMSTEADS

Navarro Vineyards & Winery
Pennyroyal Farm
PHILO and BOONVILLE

The Apple Farm
PHILO

Double 8 Dairy
PETALUMA

Green String Farm
PETALUMA

Hog Island Oyster Company
MARSHALL

Point Reyes Farmstead Cheese Company
POINT REYES STATION

Gospel Flat Farm
BOLINAS

Harley Farms Goat Dairy
PESCADERO

Pie Ranch
PESCADERO

Swanton Berry Farm
DAVENPORT and PESCADERO

Good Land Organics
GOLETA

Hilltop & Canyon Farms
CARPINTERIA

NAVARRO VINEYARDS & WINERY

Philo and Boonville

. . . .

IF YOU VISIT:

Hours: Tasting room 10 to 6 (5 in winter)

Info: navarrowine.com, sales@navarrowine.com
707-895-3686 or 800-537-9463
5601 Highway 128, Philo

Farm Tours: 10:30 and 2; reserve online

Pennyroyal Farm

Info: pennyroyalfarm.com, 707-895-2410
14930 Highway 128, Boonville

Farmstand: Tasting room under construction

Farm Tours: email sales@pennyroyal.com

Events: See website

A Family That Farms Together

Steering a battered four-wheel drive up a narrow, windy, one-lane dirt road, coffee splattering, Deborah Cahn says with a cheery laugh: "It's an insane way to farm; right?" The terraced hills make good use of the different microclimates on the approximately 1000-acre property at Navarro Vineyards, which go a long way to producing a delicious drop of wine.

Navarro was one of the first vineyards in what is now an established wine region in the fog-shrouded Anderson Valley in cool-climate Mendocino County. The Northern California winery, less than three hours north of San Francisco, is perhaps best known for its dry aromatic white wines, such as gewürztraminer, pinot gris, and riesling.

Four decades into this wine business, the winery has a loyal following. But it took a while for these niche winemakers to win over consumers. Cahn and her husband converted wine lovers one bottle at a time in direct sales from the farm.

This is pinot country, too, so the vineyard produces pinot noir wines as well. It's a sought-after sip: pinots here are known for their delicate, fruit-forward flavor. Their taste varies depending on where in the vineyard they are planted: the valley floor is temperate; the hill vineyards see cooler days and warmer nights.

Ninety acres of the former sheep ranch is planted with grapes. About half the combined acreage is planted with pinot noir vines, gewürztraminer accounts for about a third, and chardonnay is the next principle variety in the ground. The vineyard has more than 150,000 vines; they are all pruned and harvested by hand.

It's a family affair. Cahn, 67, handles accounting and administrative matters, and the bulk of the vineyard's sales and marketing. The direct sales model, which accounts for 90 percent of their business, meant Cahn wasn't away a lot on the road when her children were young.

"I wanted to be there for 4-H and soccer, and I wanted to help get our new business off the ground," says Cahn.

Husband Ted Bennett, 78, can still be found on the crush pad. But the pair isn't picking grapes at 2 a.m. like their daughter Sarah Cahn Bennett, 35, and the mother of a three-year-old and year-old twins. Son Aaron, 38, is the resident computer whiz: he handles the web-based aspects of the business.

There was no pressure to come back to the farm from the parents. "I worked quite hard to make sure the kids didn't feel like that they had to take on the vineyard," says Cahn. "But from an early age, Sarah wanted to work with animals, and Aaron came back when the time felt right."

On-the-Job Training from an Early Age

Sarah earned a masters degree in viti-culture and enology from UC Davis. She works alongside her dad and wine-maker Jim Klein. "I grew up working in the winery; I always knew I wanted to come back," she says. "As with most family businesses, I get to do a bit of everything: I make wine, I work in the vineyard, and I drive the forklift."

Sarah was raised on the farm, her parents were not. They were Berkeley dwellers, immersed in the emerging food and wine scene of that town, when they decided to become back-to-landers after Bennett sold his partnership in the successful audio chain Pacific Stereo.

They purchased the property in 1973, produced their first wines in 1975, and released their first estate wines in 1979. They've since clocked countless hours as farmers and vintners. Asked what they knew about wine making in the beginning, Cahn matter-of-factly admits: "We knew zip, zero. We were committed wine enthusiasts, and we had a game plan: to learn on the job. We figured out pretty quickly that making wine is both an art and a science."

They were also committed to farming sustainably and organically. The vineyard uses no synthetic insecticides or herbicides. Vineyard rows are banded with flowering cover crops and abuzz with beneficial insects. And their animal-loving daughter brought animals back to the ranch, which employs Babydoll Southdown sheep to graze on the farm. They serve as non-fossil-fuel-spewing mowers and fertilize the vines, too.

The family's winemaking techniques are both traditional and modern. French oak barrels are in use, as are temperature-controlled stainless steel containers. Winemakers punch down fermenting red wines by hand; it's a labor intensive way of assuring that the bright flavors of the grapes don't get lost in processing. The practice preserves tannins without causing the bitterness of the grape seeds from impacting the wine.

Navarro Vineyards' non-alcoholic wine is a big hit with drinkers of all ages and is nothing like grocery store grape juice. Bennett and Cahn first began making the alcohol-free wine for their own children. It is crafted from quickly pressed, chilled, and filtered grapes, whose juices are prevented from fermenting. "The kids loved the juice and it was a no-brainer for us. But it took Ted saying to me, 'Why are you buying the kids grape juice at the store?' before it occurred to us," says Cahn.

The farm provides permanent, full-time jobs with benefits to 60 employees, some of whom have been with the family for years; there are even second-generation employees. The vineyard produces about 45,000 cases a year, so it's bigger than a boutique vineyard but by no means an industry giant. Staying small has suited them: they have never wanted to compromise for shareholder interests, and they've enjoyed cultivating out-of-the-ordinary varieties.

Creating a Following from the Ground Up

Cahn and Bennett were creative in attracting a customer base for their wines. They started a wine club, one of the first in the country. And they clearly have fun with the farm, including the newsletter that they have written together for the past three decades. Cahn met Bennett when she was working on her graduate degree in literature at UC Berkeley; their courtship, she says, played out over meals at Chez Panisse.

The winery has seen hard times. A 2008 fire damaged a lot of the vineyard's wines, which they sold under a second label for a markedly reduced rate. The subsequent dip in the economy only made matters worse. "It was a disastrous year; humbling," recalls Cahn. But the family has bounced back and stayed true to their mission, regardless of fickle whims in the wine world.

Sarah Cahn Bennett: Vineyard farmer, winemaker, sheep herder, goat wrangler, and cheese producer.

The latest family project is Pennyroyal: a solar-powered animal farm, creamery, and vineyard in neighboring Boonville, 10 minutes down the highway. Essentially Sarah's baby, the 100-acre property features very pretty goats and sheep, each with their own names. Current handcrafted cheeses include Laychee, a soft, fresh, chevre-like goat and sheep's milk cheese, and Bollie's Mollies, a surfaced-ripened aged cheese.

Wine and cheese, right? It just made sense. There's a generosity of spirit that tends to come with the territory of running a vineyard. "We produce a product that brings people pleasure," says Cahn. "Our goal has always been to make excellent wine at reasonable prices in a way that allowed us to have the kind of lifestyle where we could stay close to our family and treat our employees well. What could be better than that?"

Recipes

New York Style Laychee Cheesecake

½ cup graham cracker crumbs
1⅓ cups sugar, divided
⅓ cup butter, melted
32 ounces Laychee (or other soft goat cheese such as chèvre)
1 teaspoon vanilla extract
4 eggs
2 cups sour cream

Mix together graham cracker crumbs, 3 tablespoons sugar, and melted butter in a bowl. Pour into a 9-inch springform pan and press into the bottom.

Cream Laychee, 1 cup sugar, and vanilla in a mixer. Add eggs, one at a time, mixing on low speed until blended. Pour over crust. Bake for 45 minutes at 350 degrees F.

While baking, mix sour cream and remaining sugar in a bowl and set aside. Once the cake is removed from the oven, pour the sour cream mixture on top, and smooth to coat evenly. Return to the oven for 10 minutes. Remove and allow to cool completely before serving.

Gewürztraminer Grape Juice Spritzer

18 seedless red grapes or red raspberries, frozen
1 bottle Gewürztraminer Grape Juice, chilled
1 liter bottle seltzer water, chilled

Divide the fruit between 6 champagne flutes. Fill the flutes half full of gewürztraminer grape juice and top with seltzer water. Stir and serve.

THE APPLE FARM

Philo

· · · · · · · · · · · · · · · · · · ·
IF YOU VISIT:

Hours: Daily, 10 to 6

Info: philoapplefarm.com, 707-895-2333
18501 Greenwood Road (at Highway 128), Philo

Farmstand: Yes. Also: Ferry Plaza Farmers Market in
San Francisco on Saturdays, August–December.

Events: For cooking stays/cottages:
philoapplefarm.com

All in the family at The Apple Farm: Karen Bates, left, and daughter Polly Bates, right.

Generational Farming

The Apple Farm is the kind of country idyll that city slickers dream of visiting. There are the orchards, of course. And there's the self-serve farmstand. There's also the well-appointed and welcoming kitchen where hands-on cooking classes take place. There's a potting shed that would make any gardener swoon.

And dotted on the property are three cottages where guests can stay overnight in California-meets-French chic countryside comfort. One cottage even overlooks the orchard, there's also a room with a view above the dining area. It's the stuff of magazine spreads.

It's also a working farm. And it's where three generations of one family has transformed a once wild and neglected apple orchard into an agricultural and culinary Eden—through getting their hands dirty, trial and error, and a little good fortune along the way.

Located in the Mendocino County hamlet of Philo, the certified biodynamic, organic Apple Farm is run by Tim and Karen Bates, aided, to varying degrees, by their daughters Sophia, Polly, and Rita. Sophia, 35, who resides on a nearby pig farm, is in charge of animal operations. Polly, 27, serves as her mom's assistant. Rita, 25, oversees the farm's row crops; her partner, Jerzy, assists in the orchards. Son Joe, 38, lives in Napa and brings his children for farm visits on a regular basis. A few full-time employees work in the fields as well, and a handful of seasonal workers help with harvest. Most days, Cruz Alvarado can be found at the stove making the farm's value-added condiments, such as preserves, using fruit sourced from the farm.

Tim Bates left a job running his own janitorial company servicing swanky restaurants in Napa Valley to take on the apple orchard. Already an avid organic gardener, the former English-literature major jumped at the opportunity to make a shift to farm life when his in-laws purchased the property. His wife Karen and her four siblings grew up around food; the couple met working at one of the family's cafes.

Karen's parents Sally and Don Schmitt ran a little restaurant called the French Laundry in the Napa Valley wine town of Yountville. Opened in 1978, it was one of the area's first set-menu restaurants serving eclectic French-inspired country cooking with a California twist. By the mid-80s it was a dining destination. In 1994, the Schmitts sold the restaurant to Thomas Keller, then a little-known chef, now a multiple-Michelin-starred celebrity. But that's another story.

The Schmitts were eager to find the next food-and-farm frontier. That brought them to the run-down apple orchard, then filled with mostly Golden and Red Delicious trees, in Philo, which is in the Anderson Valley. The area reminded these trailblazers of the Napa Valley before it transformed into *the* Napa Valley. For ten years the French Laundry subsidized the farm. Sally taught hands-on cooking courses in the farm's kitchen, aided by Karen, who has since taken over that responsibility.

"Food has always been a big part of my life: my family had the first espresso machine in the Napa Valley," says Karen Bates, now 60, who oversees guest relations, landscaping, and construction projects on the farm. "I've done everything from plastering restaurant walls to waiting tables, to working in the kitchen, to tending the restaurant garden. You learn quickly on the job. Restaurants and farms are similar in that way: there are jobs that need to get done, and everyone gets in and helps make that happen."

Restoring an Orchard

Initially, the farm needed a lot of TLC to bring it back to life. Tim Bates transitioned the farm from conventional to organic production, and soon after moved to biodynamic farming practices.

What exactly is biodynamic farming? It considers a farm as a complete organism and integrates practices that are mindful of nature's rhythms. For instance, the Apple Farm uses only local products when enhancing soil, including horse and cow manure, compost, and cover crops. Farm animals are rotated through the orchard as needed to aerate the soil and control weeds. Irrigation water comes courtesy of the nearby Navarro River and is used sparingly. This reliable water source helps provide a consistent crop, which is key to the farm's sustainability. "Our goal is to have no off-farm inputs; we'll probably never get there, but it's something to strive toward," says Karen Bates.

The key to happy apple trees, Tim Bates learned early on in his orchard education, is nutrient-dense compost. For years he used sulfur to keep fungal diseases at bay; it's a natural, if unpleasant, element that can cause farmers' eyes to itch. Now he's experimenting with neem oil to do the same job without the irritation. So far, it seems to work. That's the thing about farm life: it's an evolving practice that requires patience and a willingness to try new things when something doesn't, or no longer, works.

Early in the farm's renaissance, Tim Bates began grafting flavorful heirloom varieties onto others. Something about bringing back old-world varieties appealed

to the novice farmer. It also turned out to be a smart and timely market move: consumer interest in heirloom apples and small-batch apple ciders has grown dramatically in recent years.

About 1,500 fruit trees are in the ground, ranging in age from a year old to more than a century. The farm sports some 80 varieties of apples, by far the orchard's largest crop, with 1,350 trees over 16 acres. Popular varieties include Ashmead's Kernel, Esopus Spitzenberg, King David, Pink Pearl, Roxbury Russett, Gravenstein, and Wickson. The family renamed the farm's Golden Delicious—it's now Philo Gold—to stand out from the pack. "There's power in a name, and we wanted to differentiate ourselves," says Karen Bates. "Consumers care where their food comes from. People specifically want to buy Philo Gold apples from our farm."

The farm also grows nine different varieties of pears, as well as peaches, persimmons, plums, and five different varieties of quince. Animals are in residence, including goats, sheep, chickens, and the odd pig. There's a large produce garden that feeds the family, stocks the farmstand, and supplies the cooking classes. The farm sits on 34 acres about 2.5 hours from San Francisco, but it's truly a world away. "It's a gorgeous, magical place, and I'm reminded of that every time I return," says Polly Bates, an aerialist/dancer/stilt-walker/acrobat who comes back from performing to help with harvest and event planning on the farm. "It's also a ton of work."

Philo Fruitlandia

The farmstand and farmers market sales make up roughly a quarter of their business. Fifty percent of the fruit is sold on the wholesale market and in direct sales to restaurants and retail stores. The remaining quarter of the crop goes into jams and other products sold on the farm.

Apples are picked by hand, packed by hand, and never waxed. Customers can sample varieties piled in old wooden crates in the farmstand, which also sells jams, chutneys, dried apple rings, hard apple cider, apple juice, apple cider vinegar, and apple cider syrup. Also in the mix: whatever is seasonal and plentiful from the garden. The stand, open more than 25 years now, functions on the honor system: customers simply weigh and pay.

Diversification has helped keep everything afloat. The farm's pasteurized apple juice, what Karen calls "our bank in the barn," can help the operation get through the leaner winter months. In the fall of 2005 she co-opened Farmhouse Mercantile on the main drag in neighboring Boonville. In addition to stocking products from the farm, the retail space features modern and retro-cool kitchenware. More recently, the family has added Farm Feast events, local fund-raising dinners dished up outside

that pair farm food with neighbors' wines and apple ciders.

Farm life is not for everyone, concedes Polly. It can be isolating, even when the farm is filled with outsiders. Small-town drama and a general lack of privacy are real concerns. So, too, are disparities among different segments of the community—seasonal workers, people who own land but don't live in the area, and folks who have lived here for decades. It's also home. A place where this farm girl is acutely aware of what's sweet, juicy, bright, and buzzy about life outdoors. "Not many people can call a place like this home," she says, "and I realize more and more, every time I leave and come back, what an honor and a privilege it is to have something like this in my life."

That makes her mom happy. "We had no expectation that the kids would come back; we've just tried to make it enticing so they want to return," she says. "There's room to play and do things that appeal to your personality. But there's also a load to bear. It's a balance."

Karen's parents, well into their 80s, are planning to spend more time staying on the farm. The family is renovating living quarters for their return. Sally Schmitt is working on a memoir/cookbook, with the help of her grand-children. That coming full circle feels good to Karen Bates as well. "The farm has always been about creating something of value that brings pleasure," she says, "and it's much more mean-ingful when you share that with your extended family and the wider community."

Recipes

MULLED APPLE CIDER

1 quart fresh-pressed apple cider
2 cinnamon sticks
1-inch of fresh ginger, peeled and thinly sliced
5 whole cloves
½ teaspoon ground nutmeg
¼ cup orange juice
rind of ½ orange (in pieces)

Combine all ingredients in a large, heavy pot and bring to a boil. Reduce heat and simmer for a minimum of 30 minutes. Pour the liquid through a mesh strainer into a second pot and serve by ladling into heat-safe mugs.

APPLE CHUTNEY

6 tart green apples, peeled, cored and coarsely chopped
½ medium-sized red onion, chopped
2 tablespoons fresh ginger, peeled and minced
1 cup orange juice
¾ cup apple cider vinegar
1 cup packed brown sugar
1½ teaspoons sea salt

Combine all ingredients in a large skillet and bring to a boil over high heat. Reduce the heat and simmer, stirring occasionally, for 55 minutes or until the liquid has evaporated. Remove from heat and allow to cool before serving.

DOUBLE 8 DAIRY

Petaluma

IF YOU VISIT:

Info: double8dairy.com, info@double8dairy.com

11205 Valley Ford Road, Petaluma

Farm Tours: By appointment only

Newbie Farmer
Develops Niche Treat

Water buffalo gelato? Yep. Just the latest dairy innovation on California's coast.

In 2013, Andrew Zlot started producing creamy gelato from water buffalo milk, almost by accident. Zlot had previously partnered with a buffalo milk mozzarella maker in neighboring Tomales. When that relationship ended, he found himself with a herd of buffalo on his hands and no clue what to do with the velvety milk the animals produce.

A chance encounter proved fortuitous. Zlot met two Mendocino County gelato makers at a party and their interaction sparked an idea. He asked if they'd try creating gelato from his water buffalo milk. The gelato makers agreed and the result proved richly delicious. The pair shared their recipe—and that's how a new farm-based business was born.

Zlot runs Double 8 Dairy with third generation butter-maker Curtis Fjelstul, a former production manager at Three Twins Ice Cream, a local favorite. This is a farm-to-freezer affair: the buffalos' barns, dairy, and creamery, where the silky gelato is made, are all within a short walking distance of each other. The name Double 8 refers to the milking parlor, a U-shaped configuration that can hold sixteen buffalo (double eight) at a time.

It's a simple operation: the water buffalo are milked in the morning, gelato is produced in the afternoon, and the animals are milked a second time. Zlot repurposed a Dryer's ice-cream truck to make his delivery rounds. "It doesn't get more artisanal farmstead than that," says the first-time farmer, who grew up in the area and returned home after years working as a hedge fund manager in Hong Kong. "I was so ready to actually do something, make something, rather than just trade," says the 47-year-old. "Running a water buffalo dairy is more work than I ever imagined, but it's very fulfilling to make something unique that people really enjoy."

Water buffalo whisperer and gelato guru, Curtis Fjelstul.

Winning over the Wary, One Taste at a Time

Current flavors include plain (known as *fior di latte*, which translates as milk's flower), as well as chocolate, hazelnut, cardamom, fennel pollen, saffron, candy cap mushroom, espresso, and Thai iced tea. Many people who haven't tasted water buffalo gelato before are initially skeptical, even wary to try the product, in Zlot's experience. But that anxiety passes once they take the plunge. "We can barely keep up with demand for our gelato," says the dairyman. "People take one bite, and they're instant fans."

Double 8 Dairy gelato was dubbed "best new American ice cream" by *Esquire* magazine in 2014. This vibrantly fresh product melts in the mouth and is a darling of fine dining Bay Area restaurants. It's been on the menu at the French Laundry; Quince, Oliveto, and Delfina currently offer the sweet treat. Select local markets also sell tubs of Double 8, and the soft-serve version at Bi-Rite Creamery in San Francisco earns rave reviews.

At $8 to $12 a pint, this is a premium product. Its price, in part, reflects the costs of a small-scale start-up. And supply is an issue: a dairy cow produces about three times as much milk as a water buffalo. But

because buffalo milk is so rich, there's no need to add cream to it, as typically happens with traditional dairy gelato. Water buffalo milk contains up to 10 percent butterfat compared with 3.5 percent butterfat from dairy cows.

Lush, Creamy Goodness

Zlot started with a dozen animals. Today, he has around 75 in his herd, thanks to imported Italian water buffalo semen, which he hopes will elevate the genetic pedigree of his herd. Currently, his 25 female milking buffalo produce around half as much as Italian breeds, he says. So there's room for improvement. His heifers produce around 35 to 40 gallons a day at Double 8.

Water buffalos have called the hills around Naples, Italy, home for more than 1,000 years. After centuries of practice, Italian farmers have buffalo dairying down. Most American water buffalo are bred for their meat and produce just enough milk for their offspring, Zlot explains. That's because the udders of these quirky creatures are sized for biological roles, not dairy production. These big-bellied bovids are known for their sensitive natures and a sound that resembles a croak, not a moo. Water buffalo originally hail from Asia, where they were domesticated thousands of years ago and are commonly associated with rice farming in China.

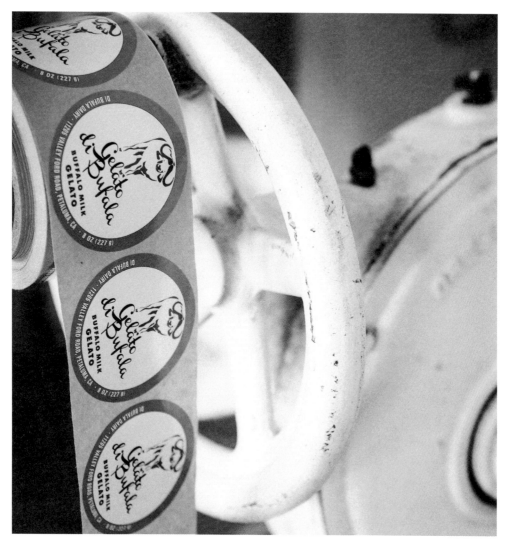

Double 8 Dairy can lay claim to making the first American water buffalo gelato on the commercial market. Not too shabby for an economics graduate who, prior to his water buffalo business, knew nothing about milking a cow, let alone a water buffalo. Zlot had never even made gelato. But he wasn't intimidated. He decided to start small, then scale up in a sustainable way, all while learning as he went. His partnership with Fjelstul, who is a co-owner, has proved invaluable.

Fjelstul is a water buffalo whisperer. He can coax milk from even the most fragile beast, says Zlot, because he's patient, kind, and persistent. A cow can produce 8 to 10 gallons of milk in five minutes whereas a water buffalo can take 15 minutes of milking to produce just 2 gallons of, granted, decadently luscious milk. Water buffalo milk

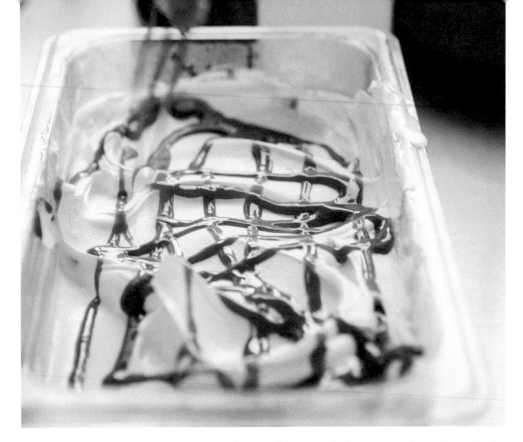

has more protein, fat, and calcium, yet less cholesterol than cow milk.

Double 8 is housed in the former cow dairy known as St. Anthony's Farm. The new owners lease the barns, pasture, and milking parlor to Zlot. There's also now a residential addiction treatment facility on the property, which was formerly the site of a Catholic Church rehab center for almost 40 years. One of its former residents, Melisa Schulze, has been a key employee at Double 8 Dairy almost since the beginning.

Producing gelato is a more efficient use of buffalo milk than making mozzarella. One gallon of milk can make 1.25 gallons of gelato. It takes four pounds of milk to make one pound of cheese. Still, Zlot hopes to be able to include mozzarella making in the farmstead's future. He also sells some water buffalo meat to area restaurants, where it has proven popular with diners.

Zlot clearly relishes his unorthodox route to farm life and the unique product he produces. "In the past, vineyard owners in the United States were told they couldn't produce great wines with American-grown grapes, and they've proved the critics wrong," he says. "Same for cheese: lots of people doubted that American dairy farmers could produce world-class cheese in the European vein. I'm up for the challenge of producing water buffalo gelato and mozzarella di bufala on par with anything made in Italy."

Recipes

CINNAMON GELATO WITH SPICED PEAR JAM COOKIES

Cinnamon Gelato:

1 tablespoon ground cinnamon
1 teaspoon salt
2 pints Double 8 *fior di latte* gelato, softened
Add cinnamon and salt to the softened gelato and
churn in an ice cream maker.
Place in the freezer until ready to serve.

Pear Jam:

5 D'Anjou pears, peeled, cored, and chopped
½ cup sugar
½ tablespoon freshly-ground black pepper
4 bay leaves
1 batch thumbprint cookies

Combine all jam ingredients in a heavy saucepan and bring to a boil for 30 minutes. Transfer the pear mixture to a blender and blend until smooth. Strain the pear mixture in a medium-gauge strainer and then refrigerate for 2 hours.

Make a batch of thumbprint cookies, using the pear jam to fill the thumbprint of the cookie.
Serve with the cinnamon gelato.

GREEN STRING FARM

Petaluma

IF YOU VISIT:

Hours: 10 to 5 daily in winter, until 6 in summer. Closed major holidays.

Info: greenstringfarm.com, 707-778-7500
3571 Old Adobe Road, Petaluma

Farmstand: Yes, the Green String Store

Farm Tours: farmtours@greenstringfarm.com

Rebel with a Cause

Bob Cannard has long had a love affair with weeds. He believes their energy is vital to keeping balance on the land. So weeds like mustard and amaranth can be found all over his Petaluma farm property in Northern California, which isn't your typical, tidy row crop operation. Cannard likes to keep things a little wild as he works with nature rather than fights against it; in the process he grows some of the most highly regarded greens around. He calls them happy, healthy plants.

"Fifty percent for nature, 50 percent for people," is his motto, meaning half his crops are grown for human consumption and half for soil improvement. Those weeds are welcome, left to grow as they please, and eventually plowed back into the ground, fertilizing the soil.

Who needs artificial inputs or chemical pesticides? Cannard raises sought-after crops in nutrient-dense dirt along with beneficial bugs. A harmonious environment allows strong crops to thrive; it's a survival-of-the-fittest situation, explains Cannard, who grew up working in his family's nursery in the same county he still lives in. He is no stranger to chemical pesticides or poisons to make plants look good for sale. And he knows firsthand how harmful they can be to human health. He learned long ago to question if plants might flourish—as they do in the natural world—without harsh interventions. His approach, while embraced by many now, was considered radical back in the day.

Cannard's harvest speaks for itself. For about 30 years, the visionary veteran farmer has served as the chief produce supplier to that temple of the farm-to-table movement, Chez Panisse in Berkeley. Founder Alice Waters handpicked Cannard, with some guidance from her dad, in what has become one of the most enduring farmer-restaurateur relationships.

Every week, seasonal bounty from Green String Farm such as pristine leafy lettuce, green garlic, squash blossoms, baby artichokes, and wild nettles can be found on the acclaimed restaurant's menu.

Unorthodox Agrarian

The 63-year-old Sonoma County farmer is a pioneer in sustainable farming circles. Cannard, who harvests a wide array of edibles, has earned his guru grower status by disregarding conventional wisdom when it comes to crop cultivation.

Over the years the unorthodox agrarian elder statesman has come to favor amending the soil with crushed volcanic rock and oyster shell mineral supplements. He's also an advocate for what he calls "compost teas," or naturally-brewed, water-based formulas that provide nutrients and help foster a self-nourishing ecosystem that requires little human intervention. His compost teas are made from ingredients like molasses, fish emulsion, rock dust, microbes, and food scraps. He's fond of working on land that's been "abused, destroyed, or allowed to die." He delights in bringing damaged soil back from the brink.

Cannard cares about his crops. He only needs to look at a plant, he says, to determine how it's feeling through its color, posture, anchorage, and size. "Plants are naked: they tell us everything about their health if we pay attention," he says. Green

String Farm, about 60 acres of cultivated land on a 150-acre property, is a produce sanctuary where a wide range of fruits and vegetables flourish under his watchful eye. "I don't like telling the plants what to do. It's better to give them a life of choice."

He doesn't stop there. As with humans, Cannard says, most physical disorders or disease in plants are associated with nutritional deficiencies. And when plants don't feel well, he maintains, they have a bad attitude and don't look, smell, or taste good. He believes gentle support helps plants become the best versions of themselves.

If his holistic approach sounds a bit woo woo for some people's tastes, Cannard-the-contrarian couldn't care less. Ditto the hungry folks who flock to his farm store on a routine basis. The Green String Store sells vibrant and fragrant herbs, glossy rainbow-colored chard with strong stems, and sweetly scented, juicy stone fruit. The tin-roofed marketplace is packed with wooden crates filled with just-picked produce, along with pantry products such as tomato sauce, honey, olive oil, walnuts, almonds, pickled beets, and preserved peppers.

Beyond Organic

Cannard uses the phrase "natural process agriculture" to describe his farming philosophy. He snorts at the label "organic" farming, deeming it "costly government paperwork stuff." The way he farms is beyond organic, he says, in terms of environmental stewardship. As the organic label has grown in popularity, it has been stripped of any real meaning, adds Cannard, who manages five other substantial garden properties in the area. He has more to say on the matter. As originally imagined, "organic" was supposed to signify local food grown with respect for the environment, using such practices as compost, cover cropping, and crop rotation, he explains. These days, organic certification is financially out of reach for many small farmers, says Cannard.

Meanwhile, big agricultural companies, he maintains, are modifying their conventional practices to garner the organic label and then shipping their produce all over the globe. The spirit of organic, says this former horticulture instructor, has been lost along the way.

He still teaches. Indeed, educating a new generation of farmers is second nature and fundamental to this lifelong man of the land. And while serious on the subject of sustainable agriculture, he's not immune to imparting his particular brand of knowledge with a mischievous smile.

Every weekday afternoon on the farm, he gives lectures to resident interns as part of the Green String Institute he cofounded in 2000 with local vineyard owner and winemaker Fred Cline.

Some lectures are on practical matters, such as irrigation issues and seed selection, others tend toward the more mystical, as is the Cannard way. Sharing what he's learned about the inherent wisdom of the wild world and understanding its role in running a healthy farm is textbook Cannard. He leaves students hungry for more.

Nurture the soil, a farm's greatest asset, is his mantra. It has been for decades. Simply put, he farms as if tomorrow matters.

Recipes

QUICK PICKLES

½ cup white vinegar
2 teaspoons sugar
1 teaspoon coarse brown mustard
1 teaspoon sea salt
1 clove garlic, diced
2 tablespoons fresh dill leaves, chopped
1 bay leaf
4 cucumbers, cut into 1-inch slices

Combine vinegar, sugar, mustard, salt, and garlic in a saucepan and simmer until the sugar dissolves. Separately combine the dill, bay leaf, and sliced cucumbers in a heat-proof bowl. Pour the simmering liquid over the cucumber mixture and stir. Chill before serving.

ROASTED ARTICHOKES WITH LEMON-THYME DIPPING SAUCE

4 artichokes
¼ cup olive oil
1 teaspoon diced garlic
2 teaspoons ground thyme
juice from ½ lemon
¼ cup mayonnaise

Scrub the outside of four artichokes, cut off the tips of the leaves with scissors, trim off the bottom of the stem, cut them into fourths, and then remove the choke from each section.

In a small bowl, combine olive oil, garlic and 1 teaspoon thyme and set aside. In a large saucepan, steam the artichoke sections for 15 minutes and then remove from the pan, place them in a single layer on a baking sheet, and brush all sides with the olive oil mixture. Bake in an oven preheated to 350 degrees F for 20 minutes or until the stems are soft when pierced with a fork. Arrange on a platter.

In a separate small bowl, combine lemon juice, mayonnaise, and remaining thyme. Whisk until creamy. Serve with the artichokes.

HOG ISLAND OYSTER
Company

Marshall

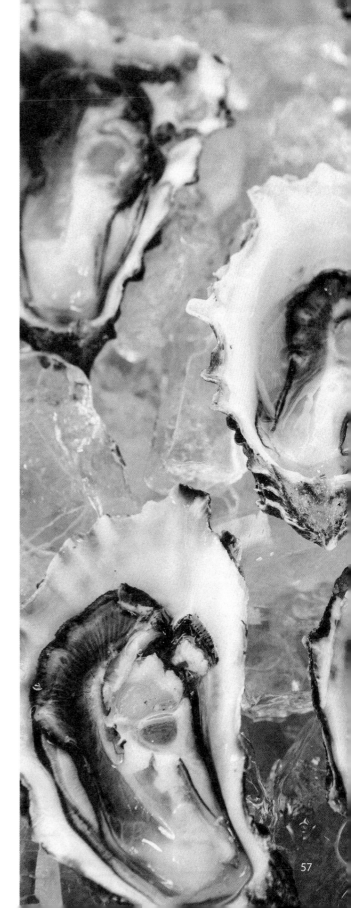

IF YOU VISIT:

Hours: Oyster Bar open Friday through Monday, 11 to 4:30

Hog Shack open daily, 9 to 5

Picnic/shuck-your-own open daily, 10 to 5, reserve in advance

Info: hogislandoysters.com, 415-663-9218

20215 Shoreline Highway, Marshall

Farmstand: Yes, the Hog Shack

Farm tours: farmtours@hogislandoysters.com

A Hit on the Half Shell

All hail the oyster farmer. Hog Island Oyster Company, the shellfish farm, was started by two marine biologists who borrowed $500 from parents and a boat from neighbors to begin cultivating coveted briny bivalves in the intertidal waters of Tomales Bay, a slender, pristine estuary about a 90-minute drive north of San Francisco.

That was more than 30 years ago. But Hog Island still has a chilled out, sea-food-shack sensibility. The laid-back vibe begins at the top with owners John Finger and Terry Sawyer, two sea dogs whose sun-weathered faces attest to lifetimes lived by the water. And yet these partners are serious stewards of the sea—and grow slurp-worthy oysters.

Hog Island oysters have quite the cult following. Finger and Sawyer preside over a $20 million operation that employs almost 200, including over 50 at the Marshall farm. The company harvests over 3.5 million oysters, clams, and mussels a year, which it sells at the farm, its popular oyster bars in San Francisco and Napa, and to select Bay Area restaurant clients. Most days of the year, oyster fans can be found on the flagship farm happily downing salty, live, raw, meaty morsels off the half shell. Hog Island's signature Pacific oysters, dubbed Sweetwaters, promise a sweet oyster liquor, smoky finish, and deep-cupped fluted shells, thanks to the rack-and-bag farming technique favored by the farm.

These shellfish farmers have shucked too many oysters to count. In the early years, the pair was out on the bay every day, with their heads down and their hands on every aspect of the oyster operation. More recently, as they both reach milestone birthdays, they're focusing on succession planning and long-term strategic thinking for the company, and scientific research and policy work for the industry. "If I can pave the way for other oyster farmers on the California coast, then that's a good thing," says John Finger, 60. "I love showing oyster growers what we do, and I love going to other oyster farms. It's a blast."

It's been hard work, of course, long hours, and unpredictable conditions. But these oystermen understand the rewards. "You get a full sensory connection to your food out here," says Terry Sawyer, also 60. "It's the smell of the sea, the look of the land, the sting of the sun and wind, the sound of the water and, of course, the taste of the ocean in our oysters. It doesn't get much better than that."

Hog Island's Matt Mackinon, shucking maestro.

Sea Stewards

Climate change is a challenge and has caused significant oyster seed shortages in recent years, in large part due to ocean acidification—climate change's caustic cousin. Overly acidic ocean conditions—courtesy of fossil fuels—are harmful to oyster shells, which need more alkaline conditions to develop their protective coverings.

Hog Island has taken a leadership role in tackling this environmental conundrum. The aquaculturalists are working with marine scientists to counter the impact this sea change has on shellfish habitat (it's responsible for killing billions of baby oysters in the Pacific Northwest, a significant source of oyster seeds for farms like Hog Island). They're also out in front on political outreach and public education.

The Hog Island crew closely monitors changes in water temperature, salinity, oxygen, and pH at the farm and adjusts to shifting conditions as needed. The farm is looking beyond science for solutions. Hog Island has

opened its own oyster hatchery in Northern California's Humboldt Bay that will provide spat, or baby oysters, for the Marshall farm and other growers. "We never thought we'd need to go into the hatchery business, but the oyster seed shortage changed that," explains Finger. The company sources them from Washington, Oregon, and Hawaii. It produces about two-thirds of the oysters it sells, and buys from East Coast and Pacific Northwest oyster farmers to round out its menu.

On any given day, some three million oysters are growing at Hog Island. The farm shoots to harvest about four million oysters per year but mortality rates are high—around 40 percent. It's an industry hazard that oyster farmers plan for. Ocean acidification doesn't help an oyster's odds of making it to the juicy size consumers have come to expect at Hog Island. But for now, these farmers are doing all they can to help this vulnerable shellfish survive and prosper.

Oyster Culture

Oysters are the ultimate sustainable seafood. They play a role in keeping seawater clean by flushing pollutants out as they feed on plankton and algae. From seed to harvest, an oyster takes about a year to grow, though waiting an additional year allows shells to deepen and harden and meat to plump up. Hog Island's Sweetwaters take about 18 months before they're ready to eat.

Hog Island's location in rural West Marin, home to small-scale dairy farms and cattle ranches, has long been protected from encroaching urban demands. The farm sits close to a land mass called Hog

SHUCK TO LIVE

Island. Little more than two acres in size, the island earned its name after a barge broke loose and left behind a posse of pigs, according to local legend.

Despite the bucolic setting, there are other pressures on its natural resources. "We have to have an awareness of what's happening with land use, too, because that impacts our farm," explains Sawyer. "We're downstream from everything that happens on the land—agriculture, cars, humans, development—it all impacts us."

The farm is an extended family affair: Terry's son helps handle the new seed operation at the Humboldt Bay hatchery; John's son is the farm manager at Marshall. Both wives play roles in the business and two of Terry's daughters work on the catering side. "We told our kids you can be on a farm crew, but you have to earn your spots," says Finger. "And we don't manage our kids; we let someone else on the team do that. It works better for everyone." There are also husband-and-wife coworkers and employees who have clocked 20 years with the company; some of their children work there, too.

Hog Island farm crewmember, Anthony Trioano, bagging bivalves.

The longtime oystermen reflect on their changing roles and a partnership that has endured. "It's been good for us to step back from the day-to-day management of the farm," says Finger. "I'm looking at big-picture policy concerns, and Terry is tackling the research end of things, which, as marine biologists, brings us back full circle to the science of what we do."

The pair knew their fascination with the sea would keep them close to the water. And they always wanted to interact with people rather than work in isolation. They've been fortunate, because of their farm and the food they produce, that the world comes to them.

And through all the ups and downs of running a farm together their friendship has never wavered. Says Sawyer: "I couldn't think of anyone else that I would have wanted to run a business with at this level—or for this long." Adds Finger: "We respect the hell out of each other; we've never questioned the other's integrity or commitment to work." And like all good friends, they remind each other to have a little fun with it, too.

Recipes

OYSTERS BARBECUED

½ cup (1 stick) butter
juice from 1 lemon
2 large cloves garlic, minced
2 dozen medium or large raw oysters
(oyster knife and fireproof gloves)

Combine all ingredients (except oysters) in a small saucepan over medium heat, and stir until the butter is melted and the ingredients are evenly combined.

Set oysters bowl-side down on a hot, charcoal grill. When the shell opens, take them off the grill (using fireproof gloves). Remove the top shell (with an oyster knife) and then set the oyster back on the grill shell side down, and spoon 1 teaspoon of the sauce over the oyster meat. Cook until the oysters are slightly caramelized.

MIGNONETTE SAUCE

½ cup shallots, minced
¼ cup white vinegar
¼ cup unseasoned rice vinegar
⅛ teaspoon sugar
⅛ teaspoon salt
2–3 dozen raw oysters, shucked
Lemon wedges

In a bowl, whisk all ingredients (except oysters and lemon wedges) together. Place shucked oysters on a platter layered with crushed ice. Add lemon wedges and hot sauce.
Serve with Mignonette Sauce.

POINT REYES

Farmstead
Cheese Company

Point Reyes
Station

· · · · · · · · · · · · · · · · · · ·

IF YOU VISIT:

Hours: By appointment only

Info: pointreyescheese.com
info@pointreyescheese.com
1-800-591-6878
14700 Highway 1, Point Reyes

Events: Farm dinners, classes, and private
gatherings at the Fork (pointreyescheese.com/thefork)

Farm Tours: Yes, by reservation

A Dad Dreams of Cheese

Once upon a time there was a dairy farmer named Bob Giacomini. He and his wife, Dean, bought a farm in 1959. They started out with 150 Holstein cows and by 1990 had about 500 animals in an idyllic setting overlooking bucolic Tomales Bay in rural West Marin. It was a lot of physical labor—tending to cows all day—and sometimes money was tight.

But farming was in Bob's bones. His grandfather, Tobias Giacomini, landed in Petaluma from Italy and began raising chickens and cows in his adopted homeland. His father, Waldo, opened his own dairy farm in Point Reyes Station in 1938. He also ran the Palace Market in town. Bob grew up helping out with the animals on the farm and unpacking boxes in the store.

Bob was born to be a dairyman. He loved the independence and working outdoors. He and Dean started a family. They raised four daughters who showed absolutely no interest in milking cows—or any other aspects of farm life. Karen, Diana, Lynn, and Jill Giacomini set off for, well, greener pastures that took them to urban settings. "The girls felt deprived growing up in the country," recalls Bob Giacomini. "They couldn't wait to get away from the farm and into the city. But the thing about greener

pastures is sometimes they start to look dried up after a while."

Jill Giacomini Basich remembers things a little differently. "We always had a deep respect and love for the land. Our mom was a farmer's daughter; she didn't want us to have the responsibility of the farm weighing on us," Giacomini Basich says. "She wanted us to pursue education and careers, to explore the world unfettered by the farm. And we did."

Fast forward a couple of decades. When farmer Bob turned 60, he and Dean gathered "the girls" around a table for a series of frank conversations. They wanted to know if their daughters had any interest in running the farm. The couple was considering retiring from the family business and looking for a buyer if the daughters weren't fazed by that decision. Farmer Bob, wearing his Dad hat, reminisced about how he'd long wanted to make a value-added product but he'd never had the people power or time to make it a reality. He dreamed of cheese. But absent extra help, he'd had to send his milk off the farm in trucks every day. Would his daughters come back to the farm, he mused, and maybe they could make a go of it? All four daughters, he says, put their hands up.

Bring on the Blue

It took the collective expertise of "the girls" and their edible entrepreneurship to make their Dad's dream a reality. As adults, the daughters had explored interests beyond their rural upbringing: Diana went into investments, Lynn had a sales background, Karen was a stay-at-home mom, and Jill worked in marketing. Three of the four daughters came back to the farm in the late 1990s, with Diana, who had a career in banking, coming on board in 2009, following the financial market crash.

They had no clue how to make cheese. And they knew nothing about food production, dairy science, or microbiology. But their professional skills, love of cooking, and fondness for the property they once called home informed their new life path. The milkman's daughters spent almost two years researching what kind of product to make.

At the time, an artisan cheese-making movement was beginning to emerge around the country. And much of it was happening in the Giacominis' backyard. "Respectfully, we didn't want to compete with our local allies," says Giacomini Basich. "In our travels across the country, when we asked what cheese was missing from the West Coast it was always blue, blue, blue. Blue cheese was a no-brainer because it works so well in so many recipes. And from a marketing perspective it was well known. We found our niche."

In 2000, the first wheels of creamy Point Reyes Original Blue debuted. They were crafted in a former horse barn that had been rebuilt as a modern cheese production creamery.

And the first sale? To the Palace Market in Point Reyes Station. For Farmer Bob, his life's work had returned to where he started. And since then, the family's award-winning, rindless, classic blue cheese has been joined by three others, which have been honored by the Good Food Awards,

Specialty Food Association, and American Cheese Society. In the mix: Bay Blue, a rinded, rustic blue cheese with a fudgy texture; a familiar, fluffy, white Mozzarella; and Toma, a buttery-flavored semihard table cheese. The company's cheese production is led by cheese-guy-in-charge Kuba Hemmerling. "For the first three years we started, we didn't take any salaries; we joke that we got paid in cheese instead," says Giacomini Basich, 45, who drives from Oakland every day to work, at least an hour-long commute.

Farmstead First

The family takes their farmstead designation to heart. "Our top core value is that we are a farmstead, which means we have total control over our raw ingredient, and we take good care and all responsibility for the milk that goes into our cheese," says Giacomini Basich. "It starts with the grasses we grow, our animal husbandry, and the feeding of our cows. We are animal humane certified and our milk is rBST free, which means it has no hormones. Our milk tastes like our land. That's our point of difference."

Bob Giacomini has long advocated on behalf of small farms. He served for six years on the National Dairy Board, two years as president. "My dad is a role model in his commitment to the environment, in his belief that a farmer and a conservationist can be one and the same," says Giacomini Basich. She adds, "He believes that land stewardship needs to be an integral part of your farming plan, that sustainability isn't a trend to follow, it's a responsibility that allows you to stay ahead of the challenges that come with farming life, many of which are beyond your control."

The dairy farm is beyond organic and uses rotational grazing, which keeps grasses and soils healthy. In 2009, the Giacominis installed a methane digester that converts methane gas—a byproduct of manure—into the useable energy that powers the dairy and cheese plant. They also compost their solid manure and sell some to a local compost company that in turn sells it to nurseries and other farmers. "Our land has been very good to us, and we consider it our duty and honor to return the favor," says Giacomini of the 700-acre property with 40 employees.

The daughters are the driving force behind the farm's custom-built facility designed with education and enjoyment in mind. Opened in 2010, the Fork offers farm tours, hands-on and demo-style culinary classes, cheese tastings, monthly farm dinners, and other events in a building that boasts a stunning, state-of-the-art instructional kitchen, dining room with communal

seating, outdoor patio, and garden. "We wanted to bring people here so they could observe our farming practices, meet our animals, see the people who make our cheese," says Giacomini Basich. "And we wanted to offer a more formalized hospitality program."

The last word on farmstead life belongs to Farmer Bob. "I love what I do. You have to: it's hard work and we run lean," says Giacomini, whose wife died in 2012. "I'm still dairy farming at 78—that says it all, really. And I got the girls back. How lucky am I?"

Recipes

FIGS WRAPPED WITH PROSCIUTTO, STUFFED WITH POINT REYES BLUE CHEESE

One dozen fresh figs
6 thin deli-style slices of Italian prosciutto,
cut in half lengthwise and fat trimmed off
3 ounces blue cheese

Rinse the figs and slice off the tops. Wrap each fig with half strip of prosciutto and then place the wrapped figs in a lightly oiled, glass baking dish. Poke your finger into the top of each fig to create a cavity and fill the hole with roughly 1½ teaspoons of blue cheese. Place into a 350 degree F oven and bake for approximately 25 minutes or until the prosciutto is slightly crisp and cheese has melted. Let cool slightly and serve.

BLUE CHEESE AND PEAR BRUSCHETTA

1 baguette, sliced into ¼-inch rounds
¼ cup olive oil
8 ounces blue cheese
2 to 3 red pears, thinly sliced

Arrange the baguette rounds on a baking sheet. Brush with olive oil, and then bake in an oven, preheated to 400 degrees F, until lightly toasted but not too crisp; approximately 8 minutes.

Spread a layer of blue cheese on the toasted baguette rounds and then top with a thin slice of pear. Serve warm or cold.

GOSPEL FLAT FARM

Bolinas

IF YOU VISIT:

Hours: 24/7

Info: gospelflatfarm.com
208 Olema Bolinas Road, Bolinas

Farmstand: Yes

Farm tours: Email: murchm@gmail.com

Art Meets Ag

For Mickey Murch, cultivating crops is a creative endeavor. Whether he's harvesting by hand or planting seeds via tractor, art and agriculture intersect at Gospel Flat Farm, where growing food is a living art form, not just a way to make a living.

Take his 24-hour Farmstand. Beloved by locals and visitors alike, the simple structure by the side of the road is the farm's permanent art installation and features a rotating display of earthy sustenance. Wooden crates boast fresh picked greens, root vegetables, and herbs. Buckets hold showy flowers. Eggs fill an assortment of baskets. Crab makes an appearance, in season. "It's a form of art to constantly interact with food," says Murch, a second-generation farmer. "There's a human power to produce and the Farmstand is an expression of collective creative forces on the land. The people who stop by and interact with the space are a part of the art, too. It's social sculpture functioning as an art form."

Gospel Flat's name is a nod to the four houses of hope that once graced the area, located a few miles from the cliff-hugging coastal Highway 1, past a tidal estuary and beyond a grove of towering eucalyptus trees. Murch is a modern-day good news man, spreading the gospel of organic farming and community connection through his farm-fresh food in this pastoral setting in West Marin a mere 30 miles north of San Francisco.

Murch had no plan to work the land as a way of life. In 2002, when he set off for Reed College in Portland, Oregon, to study conceptual and environmental art, he never imagined he'd eventually come home to run the family farm in Bolinas. And yet his college art reflected his upbringing. Murch splashed paint on work boots and wheelbarrows. He lived rough for a year, exploring whether a student could survive on campus by growing, making, finding, recycling, or bartering basic necessities. He camped out in a handmade rolling caravan and stitched shoes from leather straps and tire treads. He preserved produce, beer, beans, cider, and salmon in Mason jars. He made an indoor exhibit that included a film documenting his experience.

Murch realized that his artistic persona was so thoroughly entwined with his farm-boy background that he made his way back to the land. In Portland, he built himself a pod to live in as part of a sculpture assignment. In 2006, he brought it back with him to Bolinas so he could better commune with the natural world.

Mickey Murch makes farming a creative practice.

GOSPEL FLAT FARM

This is a family farm
We live here, so please
smile and say hello.

His creative pursuits with an edible bent continued. Murch fashioned a mobile kitchen out of an old boat, which he hitched onto a trailer and towed into town, bringing the farm to the people. The boat serves as a portable classroom of sorts, educating children about canning fresh food or pressing apples for cider. Local chefs have borrowed the boat for pop-up dinners with a homegrown, artsy feel.

A Family Affair

Farming on the edge appeals to this child of the eclectic coastal enclave affection-ately known by residents as Bobo. Mickey Murch's parents, Don Murch and Sarah Hake, moved to Gospel Flat Farm in 1980. Murch senior and the family transformed the site, blighted from a decade of trash buildup, into fields of organic greens.

After graduating, Murch junior took over the day-to-day operations of man-aging the farm while Don, a lifelong fisherman, focused on his heavy-equipment business. The two Murch men take care of the crab pots together. Mickey's brother Kater kicked off the family's on-site wine production. His mom, a university plant geneticist, bakes bread in the outdoor

wood-fired oven. His maternal grandmother is a painter and has her own art studio on the farm.

The 32-year-old Murch lives on the farm with wife Bronwen and their three young children. His family shares the big Victorian house on the property with his parents. Bronwen curates events at a barn Mickey built behind the Farmstand, which serves as a revolving showcase for other artists' work.

In the early days, the younger Murch made typical first-time-farmer mistakes. It took a few growing seasons to figure out what produce to grow and where, as he got to know intimately the climatic conditions of the farmland. Even something as simple as watering crops has a learning curve. "A new farmer will look at the surface soil and see that it's dry, but a seasoned grower will kick down the soil a few inches to check for moisture," he says.

He didn't have any idea how to sell what he grew. He just knew he didn't want to have to drive "over the hill" to San Francisco to sell his bounty. He tried delivering produce boxes and inviting people to the farm to pick their own, but neither felt quite

right. Almost as an afterthought, he began putting excess vegetables by the side of the road. That proved the inspiration for the Farmstand. The unattended stand works on the honor system; customers weigh and pay without oversight. The locked money box is emptied regularly.

Murch enjoys fielding questions from folks who stop by. A favorite: "What do you do with *this*?" He relishes introducing eaters to unfamiliar produce, such as a root vegetable he refers to as a snow apple. It's actually a Japanese turnip, a crisp, white globe of surprising sweetness that can be eaten raw. And he enjoys not having to haggle with wholesalers over the price or appearance of his produce. "You can accomplish so much when you don't have to peddle your wares," says the farmer, who most days tends his 10 acres with the help of two employees. Murch does the bulk of the tractor work, his fellow farmers, originally from Mexico, harvest crops and stock the stand.

Farmstand Success

Murch's faith in farming has paid off. The Farmstand not only feeds Murch's creative needs, it's economically viable. He makes more money from the stand, he says, than he would selling wholesale or at farmers markets and is able to support a family of five.

The stand has been running for almost 10 years and has served as a model for similar small farms elsewhere in the Golden State.

Murch takes being a good husband to the land to heart and innovates farming in multiple ways. Beginning in 2011, he leased four acres of neighboring public land for dry-farm cultivation, a drought-friendly farming practice that requires little or no irrigation. The reclaimed area, long neglected, has become a key part of the small farm's year-round production of produce, including arugula, beets, fava beans, tomatoes, and spinach.

While what he manifests starts with seeds in the soil, it comes to fruition at the table. "We want the food we grow to inspire people to cook and gather to eat," he says. "When art, farming, food, care for the land, and creativity in the kitchen come together to form community, it's a beautiful thing." Spoken like a true artist-farmer.

Recipes

CHIMICHURRI SAUCE

½ cup fresh parsley

1 cup fresh cilantro

¼ cup fresh basil

½ cup olive oil

¼ cup balsamic vinegar

2 garlic cloves, peeled

1 teaspoon crushed red pepper

½ teaspoon fine sea salt

Place all the ingredients in a food processor and puree. Transfer to a bowl, cover, and let stand at room temperature for 2 hours, stirring occasionally, to allow the flavors to meld.

HONEY-GLAZED SNOW APPLES
(also called Japanese turnips)

2 cups snow apples, tops removed, cleaned and sliced (*no need to peel*)

3 tablespoons organic honey

2 tablespoons organic coconut oil

2 pinches sea salt

Mixed greens (*optional*)

Balsamic vinaigrette (*optional*)

Fresh mint sprigs (*optional*)

Place the sliced turnips in a skillet and add water until the turnips are just covered. Add honey, coconut oil, and salt; stir together and then bring the mixture to a boil. Continue boiling until the turnips are tender and the honey mixture has thickened to the consistency of syrup.
Remove from heat and serve warm either tossed with mixed greens and balsamic vinaigrette or garnished with sprigs of fresh mint.

HARLEY FARMS GOAT DAIRY

Pescadero

IF YOU VISIT:

Hours: Daily 10 to 5

Info: harleyfarms.com
650-879-0480
205 North Street, Pescadero

Farmstand: Yes, cheese shop

Farm Tours: Yes, by reservation

Events: Seasonal dinners

Poor Man's Cow
Proves Popular

Deborah (Dee) Harley didn't raise animals as a child. Her father had an allergy to fur, so she grew up without pets in a small coal-mining village in rural Yorkshire in Northern England. There was no inkling in her formative years that Harley would pursue a life devoted to the care, feeding, and milking of livestock. But from a young age she knew she wanted to be a farmer, leading a rural, outdoor life.

These days, Harley's a goat-wrangling expert with decades of experience under her belt. On her 1910 property, Harley Farms Goat Dairy, she tends to some 200 American Alpine goats which gambol about in groups in the pastures. The bucolic setting also includes a donkey, three llamas, a couple of dogs, a few cats, and 40 chickens.

Harley had wanderlust as a teenager. She left home at 17 and never really went back. Her travels brought her to Pescadero, where she befriended a local character called Three-Finger Bil, a folk artist and woodworker whose creations are featured at Harley Farms. And she fell in love with her now-husband Tim Duarte, who still runs his family's local restaurant down the road, the iconic Duarte's Tavern known for its artichoke soup and olallieberry pie.

In the late 1980s, the couple bought the 12-acre former cow dairy whose barn and milking parlor were in disrepair. It hadn't been a working dairy since the 1950s, but the location couldn't be beat. This country enclave just 45 minutes south of San Francisco is minutes from some of the most picturesque—and relatively undeveloped—Pacific coastline in California. The area has a rich agricultural history: dairy farms were once widespread here. Harley rather liked the idea of bringing the farm back to life again.

In 1990, Nancy Gaffney, a local cheesemaker, suggested Harley overwinter six of her goats. A few years later, when Gaffney retired from the goat game, Harley ended up with all of her herd and her cheesemaking operation as well. Harley's had her share of ups and downs over the years, like any farmer, but she considers it a privilege to work the land. "We get a lot of visitors to the farm; people really feel something special when they come here. They fall in love with the animals, and they're respectful of the effort that's gone into restoring the place," says the 49-year-old.

It's been a work in progress. With help from the California Coastal Rural Development Corporation—which provided a timely low-interest $50,000 loan slated for minorities (including women) in agriculture—she refurbished existing infrastructure and

Goat wrangler, Dee Harley.

purchased new equipment. Harley asked Salud and Roberto Zavala, whom she had worked with at nearby Jacobs Farm, to come help care for her goats and learn the cheese-making business.

White Gold

The farm's goat cheese has proven popular with critics and consumers. Salud Zavala uses traditional cheese-making methods, such as separating curds and whey with cheesecloth bags, in the production process. The farm is one of a small number of goat cheese producers in the country who raise their own animals and use their own goat milk, says Harley. That allows them to control quality and maintain consistency. "It's a true farmstead dairy," she says. About 200 pounds of goat cheese is made on the farm every day. The farm's milk is pasteurized, and while not certified organic, the goats are fed hay, grain, and fresh pasture and receive no antibiotics or hormones.

Happy goats make good cheese and farm first are the guiding principles at the dairy. Animal welfare and wholesome feed are

top priorities here. Each goat produces about a gallon of milk a day, and a gallon of milk makes about one pound of cheese. The farm breeds its own goats in the fall; babies arrive in late February through May, a favorite time for visitors to watch gangly, fluffy, horn-free kids frolic in the fields.

Judging by accolades alone, they're doing something right on the cheese front. The farm produces award-winning goat cheeses, including chevre, fromage blanc, feta, and ricotta. Harley's edible-flower-festooned wheel of goat cheese, dubbed Monet, won gold at the World Cheese Awards in 2014. The cheeses are consistent American Cheese Society winners, with 20 national ribbons and counting.

True to its farmstead roots, the cheeses are sold on site. Some rounds are infused with savory flavorings such as garlic and herbs, or sun-dried tomato and basil; others offer sweet notes such as honey and lavender; chocolate and raspberry; or apricot and pistachio. There's a salt-brined feta that's so popular the farmer calls it white gold.

The farm shop also sells soaps and body lotions made from goat milk. Harley even offers a line of goat-milk-based paints in nine bright colors; FarmPaint is biodegradable, contains natural pigments, and boasts a suede-like finish.

The shop was born out of necessity: strangers frequently knocked at Harley's door wanting to buy her goat cheese. She wanted a bit more privacy. What started with a money jar and a basket of goat cheese by the back door has turned into a busy retail spot.

The farmstead is a hodgepodge of structures that add to the property's charm. A small wooden house, where Harley raised her son, sits adjacent to a flower-filled garden bursting with vibrant colors. The barn houses the creamery, retail outlet, and a private dining room in the repurposed hayloft.

Adjacent to the barn is a milking parlor and a sheltered "loafing" barn, where goats come to chill out after playing and grazing in the pastures. Given her background, it's not surprising that the farm has an English village dairy aesthetic—eucalyptus trees, Pacific Coast fog, and Northern California sunshine notwithstanding. "This is a small, connected community with plenty of space to breath," says Harley.

About 30 people, not all full-time, work at the farm. Locals lead the goat tours: The town's high school principal calls her Sunday tours "church;" other regular guides include a financial planner, and a teacher who works with special-needs children, some of whom help out on the farm, too.

The Secret Garden

In 2011, Harley bought 20 acres of neighboring fields. She calls it the secret garden. There's an orchard and more than 25 beehives, which are tended by local beekeepers Gary and Teri Butler, who have 400 hives along the coast. Their "hobby on steroids," as Teri Butler calls it. The Butlers' honey is sold under the label Half Moon Honey. The Harley Farms honey, unlabeled, can be purchased from the farm's store. "It's a great location for hives—there are apple and quince trees, it's close to a creek (bees drink lots of water), and there are four acres of berries nearby," says Harley.

The garden is a sought-after location for weddings and other special occasions. Harley doesn't just espouse a hoof-to-harvest philosophy, she lives it. The table, chairs, and plates that are used at the farm's meals

are handmade and sourced locally. Much of the produce for these dinners come from the farm's own garden.

The best part of Harley's day? "Nothing beats looking out of the kitchen window, with a cup of coffee in hand, watching the goats go out to pasture together and start chomping on that lovely green grass," she says. "It's quite a satisfying vision. We really do live and breathe the farm. But that devotion has been rewarded in so many ways."

Recipes

GOAT CHEESE–CRUSTED LAMB CHOPS

4 lamb chops
3 shallots, minced
3 sprigs rosemary, finely chopped
3 tablespoons lavender, finely chopped
¼ cup water
¼ cup Dijon mustard

Combine all ingredients (except Dijon mustard and lamb chops) in a blender and blend until pureed. Place the lamb chops in a large zip-lock bag, add the herb mixture to the bag, and shake to evenly coat the chops. Place in the refrigerator for 2 hours. Remove the lamb chops from the marinade bag and brush them with Dijon mustard and set aside.

Goat Cheese Crust:

3 cups toasted sourdough bread crumbs
½ pound chèvre goat cheese, crumbled
1 tablespoon olive oil

Combine bread crumbs and goat cheese in a bowl and mix until ingredients form a coarse crumble. Remove the lamb chops from the marinade and press the goat cheese mixture onto both sides. Add oil to a hot skillet and sear the lamb chops until light brown on both sides and then bake in a 350 degree F oven for 15 minutes or until desired doneness is achieved.

HONEY ALMOND GRANOLA

1 cup chopped almonds
3 cups old fashioned rolled oats
¼ cup brown sugar
½ teaspoon sea salt
⅓ cup organic honey
3 tablespoons organic coconut oil
½ teaspoon vanilla extract
¼ teaspoon almond extract

Preheat the oven to 350 degrees F and line a baking sheet with parchment paper. In a large bowl, mix together the almonds, oats, and sea salt. Next, in a small microwave-safe bowl, combine the honey and coconut oil and then microwave for 30 seconds or until the mixture becomes a warm liquid. Stir and then add the vanilla extract and almond extract to the honey mixture. Pour the combined liquid ingredients into the oat mixture and stir until the dried ingredients are evenly coated. Pour the oat mixture onto the parchment-lined baking sheet and spread evenly. Bake for five minutes, stir and re-spread the mixture, and then continue baking an additional five minutes. Allow to cool thoroughly then break into clusters.

PIE RANCH

Pescadero

· ·

IF YOU VISIT:

Hours: Mon., Wed., Thurs. & Fri. 12 to 6 p.m.,
Saturday & Sunday 10-6. Closed Tuesdays.

Info: pieranch.org, 650-879-0995
2080 Highway 1, Pescadero

Farmstand: Yes

Farm Tours: Yes

Events: Workday, potluck, and barn dance on third
Saturday of the month

Partners in life and on the farm: Nancy Vail and Jered Lawson.

Sharing the Pie

Who doesn't love pie? In 2002, Nancy Vail and Jered Lawson, along with a third cofounder, purchased a 14-acre farm property in Pescadero with the intention of helping people understand where their food comes from through sustainable farming and hands-on education.

They dubbed the land Pie Ranch, because of its wedge-shaped nature, and because pie seemed a pretty good way to whet people's appetites for learning. The pair is also partial to the idea of "pie-in-the-sky" innovation for collective good.

The social-change advocates, partners in life and on the land, struck a chord with pie lovers of all ages. Since 2005, when Pie Ranch officially began operating as a working farm, they have sought to connect the local community with the land—one scrumptious slice at a time.

The old barn at the beginning of the property welcomes visitors with fresh-picked organic greens, tree fruit, berries, eggs, and flowers. And, of course, the stand carries just-baked pies such as strawberry-rhubarb, lemon-buttermilk, and walnut, which come courtesy of Companion Bakeshop in nearby Santa Cruz and feature ingredients from the farm.

More than a decade later, there's nothing half-baked about this growing nonprofit farmstead. Given its name, it's not surprising that the farm grows crops that are key to making a mouthwatering pie: berries, rhubarb, apples, pumpkins, eggs, and wheat. Pies are the lure the farmers use to hook folks to come to the farm, says Lawson. But visitors rapidly come to appreciate the joys and benefits of cooking from scratch with real whole food.

"We use pie as a metaphor for everything when teaching students about the current state of our food system," adds Vail. For instance, they talk about who has a slice of the pie and who doesn't have access to healthy and organic food, and how that can be addressed in a more equitable system. "We have high ideals for making the world a better place," she says. "Through food and farming, we are utilizing principles of health, sustainability, and justice for really pie-in-the-sky changes that are so necessary in our society."

The farm draws about 40,000 visitors a year. At Pie Ranch's well-equipped, open-air kitchen, hundreds of youth have baked pies. Still, these field trips, geared toward teenagers—many of whom have never set foot on a farm—aren't just about eating a slice of deliciousness. There's instruction on sound eating and sustainable farming, plus the chance to get their hands dirty.

Cultivating Community

A monthly community workday, potluck, and barn dance—break out the flannel shirts, boots, and ranch hats—brings adults, families, university students, urban farm-friendly hipsters, and children to the farmstead. The ranch offers a one-year apprenticeship and a summer internship program in partnership with three local high schools called HomeSlice.

The programs allow youth to dig a little deeper, in exploring such matters as food justice. Pie Ranch is a Food Justice Certified farm. "We watch students gain skills, confidence, and a sense of joy and wonder about the natural world when they have the opportunity to nurture plants, harvest crops, learn scratch cooking, and share this knowledge with their peers around the table," says Lawson. "It's meaningful stuff."

The couple met through local farming circles. Friends for years, their romance began in 2001 at EcoFarm, an annual conference on the California coast for committed alternative agriculture types. Vail, 46, and Lawson, 45, live on the land in a 700-square-foot yurt in the rear of the Pie Ranch property with their two young children, Lucas, 10, and Rosa, 9. It's clear these family farmers enjoy working together but also carve out opportunities to connect on interests beyond the farm. When time allows, they pursue their own hobbies:

Lawson is an avid surfer, Vail plays fiddle, including in the barn dance band the Country Line Pickers.

Today, Pie Ranch encompasses 27 acres—the original piece of land named the Upper Slice features assorted fruit trees, leafy greens, root vegetables, and livestock such as chickens, goats, and a cow. The Lower Slice is home to the ranch's popular farmstand, educational classroom, and historic structures. Like many small farms, Pie Ranch has a robust CSA (community-supported agriculture) program with local residents. It's a joint commitment: community members sign on to buy farm produce for a season or in some cases year-round, which provides farmers with an economically secure base for their bounty. In return, farmers agree to grow delicious, nutritious, high-quality produce at a competitive price.

CSA 2.0

There's more. In 2014, the farm began a pilot project called Pie Ranch at Año Nuevo, on land across the highway from the farmstand. Here, Pie Ranch leases 75 acres, where they grow a range of vegetables, grains, and legumes. Think wheat, barley, peas, fava beans, brassicas, and dark leafy greens. In the near future, the site, formerly

Farmstand Manager, Tamar Ingber, keeps track of inventory.

a longtime flower farm, will become home to pasture-raised animals. Pie Ranch is also an animal-welfare approved farm. It's a program that raises the farm's profile in the sustainable, small-scale farming landscape. And they're playing with a new CSA model to ensure its success. Lawson calls it CSA 2.0.

It's a high-profile undertaking. Pie Ranch has partnered with Google Food and Stanford University Dining on the project. In this case the institutions, rather than individuals, front production funds, committing to crops that are destined for the dining facilities on these two campuses. For Pie Ranch, this means scaling up and bringing their food to thousands of new customers. As the program evolves, individual Google employees and Stanford faculty and students will be able to purchase shares in the new economic model Pie Ranch calls "Farm to Firm to Family."

Next step: to partner with local school districts, including San Francisco Unified, on the project. "It's great that these powerful and privileged organizations have supported us. We also want to reach a diverse group of young eaters—and not just through school cafeterias," says Vail. "We are developing a meal-kit concept where students can take food home to their families and cook together."

Pie Ranch continues to look for ways to make sure everyone gets a slice of the pie. Case in point: a Relearning Garden in

partnership with the Amah Mutsun Tribal Band and Land Trust is in the works. As conceived, the space will serve the Native American original residents of this land and the public, providing historical context and interactive activities with native plants as the lens, says Vail.

At Pie Ranch, raising the next generation of farmers is front and center to its mission. "What could be more important to the planet, human survival, and community building than creating a healthier food system?" asks Vail. Lawson adds that it's the future farmers who "are going to advocate for preserving local farmland and grow food with love and care. You can't put a price tag on teaching youth about the importance of that."

There is a sense of urgency at Pie Ranch on this subject. "There's this beautiful tradition of small family farming on the coast that's quietly and rapidly disappearing," says Lawson. "All this collective knowledge around soil, water, and climate that's gone into raising crops for a really long time. We want to do what we can to ensure that continues."

Recipes

BLACKBERRY PIE

Crust for two-crust 9-inch pie
6 cups fresh organic blackberries
1 cup sugar
2 tablespoons butter, melted
2 teaspoons lemon juice
zest from one medium lemon
1 egg, lightly beaten
Extra granulated sugar for sprinkling

Preheat oven to 400 degrees F and place a baking sheet on the lower rack. Line a pie plate with one of the two rounds of pie crust and trim the edges, leaving ½ inch overhang. In a large bowl, combine berries, sugar, butter, lemon juice, lemon zest, and gently stir until evenly mixed then pour berry mixture into the pie pan lined with pie crust. Roll out remaining piece of dough into a 9-inch round. Lay the crust over the filling, roll up and crimp edges then make three 1-inch cuts out of the top crust. Brush top and edge with egg and sprinkle all over with sugar. Bake on hot baking sheet until crust is golden brown and filling is bubbling, approximately 1 hour to 1 hour and 10 minutes. Cool pie before serving to allow juices to thicken.

WALNUT PIE

Crust for one-crust 9-inch pie
1 cup dark corn syrup
½ cup sugar
3 large eggs
2 tablespoons unsalted butter, melted
1½ tablespoons all purpose flour
2 teaspoons vanilla extract
¼ teaspoon salt
1½ cups walnut pieces

In a large bowl, combine syrup, sugar, eggs, butter, flour, vanilla, salt and whisk until smooth. Add the walnuts and stir until mixed thoroughly. Line a pie pan with the pie crust, roll and trim the edges. Poke the tines of a fork into the crust several times to keep air pockets from forming under the crust. Pour the walnut mixture into the crust and bake in a preheated oven at 350 degrees F for 55 minutes or until the center is set. Cool pie completely before serving.

SWANTON BERRY FARM

Davenport and Pescadero

Swanton Berry Farm owner and farm workers' rights advocate, Jim Cochran.

now part of a research trial of farms experimenting with growing starter strawberry plants free from toxic-fumigant-treated soil. A little known fact: California—one of the world's largest strawberry-growing regions—has only one commercial-scale organic strawberry plant nursery source. Out of business for a few years, it is expected to be up and running again in 2016, according to Cochran. It's not enough for Cochran to grow some of the sweetest, juiciest Chandler strawberries on the Central Coast, and make progress on the growing end. A product of a cooperative-friendly bygone era (Cochran worked for a conventional strawberry production co-op in the 1970s), he wants to do the right thing by his employees, too.

In 1998, Swanton's became the first strawberry farm in the United States to sign a contract with the United Farm Workers. Cochran and fellow co-owners are labor union supporters: they pay workers a fair wage and offer paid vacation, health insurance, and other benefits. In 2006, the farm went further and began offering an employee stock-ownership plan, likely the first such program in U.S. agriculture production. "Just as organic certification formalizes our commitment to growing practices that are good for the environment, our union contract and stock ownership

Food Justice Leader

Strawberry grower Jim Cochran clearly enjoys his maverick status. Cochran's Swanton Berry Farm has a lot of firsts attached to his operation. For starters, Swanton's was the first farm in California to grow commercial organic strawberries. Cofounded by Cochran in 1983, Swanton's became certified organic in 1987. "People in the strawberry-growing business thought I was stupid; the modern way to do things was to use pesticides," says Cochran, 68, a farmer for almost four decades. "I proved them wrong."

The farm continues to innovate on the berry-farming front: Swanton's is plan formalizes our commitment to the human side of the farming equation," says Cochran. Swanton Berry Farm employs around 25 full-time and another 10 or so part-time seasonal workers.

The leader-of-the-pack status doesn't end there. In 2014, Swanton was acknowledged by the Agricultural Justice Project as a farm demonstrating high social-justice standards. The Food Justice Certified label, awarded by a nonprofit coalition concerned with domestic fair-trade matters, has so far been granted to only a handful of the nation's farms. For Cochran, growing wholesome produce and nurturing farmworker dignity go hand-in-hand in the quest for an equitable food system for everyone.

All this is behind-the-scenes stuff: many strawberry lovers simply know the farm as a great place to harvest their own berries, pick up a punnet or two or three of overflowing, aromatic ruby red orbs, or grab a couple of jars of their luscious preserves. Strawberry-olallieberry, blackberry, tayberry, loganberry, or strawberry-rhubarb jam sound good?

Kicking Chemicals

The farmstead setting couldn't be more charming: Swanton leases 80 acres of coveted California coastline, at Coastways in Pescadero. The farmstand sits on 50 acres permanently preserved thanks to the Trust for Public Land. Cochran has never had to worry that a developer was going to pave paradise and put up a parking lot.

Cochran grew up in Southern California in Carlsbad, which then featured pockets of farm country. He attended college in the 1960s at the University of California, Santa Cruz, where he became interested in unconventional farming practices. Nevertheless, he began his commercial farming career growing strawberries using conventional methods. After first-hand exposure to the harmful health impact of poisonous pesticides, however, he vowed to find a different way to farm.

Strawberries are a fragile, finicky fruit. Cochran's primary tools for pest management and soil health: crop diversity and soil building. The farmers spend several years building up the soil with compost before planting strawberries. They also rotate field crops, such as subbing in broccoli or

cauliflower, to help control disease and pests.

Once a lone voice in the organic strawberry business, Cochran's farm has influenced many California farmers who now grow organic berries, Swanton style. Seeing his success, even some of the biggest berry producers in the country have followed suit. Since the 1960s, conventional California strawberries have been grown with the aid of a highly toxic soil fumigant called methyl bromide. The chemical, banned for years in most of the developed world, is slated to be fully phased out of the United States by the end of 2016, ending a decades-long chemical dependency by strawberry farmers.

Unlike large agribusiness crops such as soy, grain, or dairy, the profit margins for a small-scale strawberry farmer are pretty thin. And there are no government subsidies to sweeten the deal. Moreover, strawberries are tricky plants, prone to fungus, pests, and weeds. Strawberry farming is not a way of life for the risk averse. But Cochran and company at Swanton's are resilient, persistent souls.

A Boom for Berries

Swanton's is no ovenight success story. Begun with a partner and just four acres of land in the Swanton Valley, the early, conventional-method years were difficult. The first few years as an organic outfit were even tougher. Yields were low; trial and error proved the order of the day. Cochran held a second job for the first six years or so, just to keep food on the table, but his growing gamble eventually paid off: production methods worked, yields improved, flavor and form began to shine, and Whole Foods came calling. These days, especially after several drought years, it's difficult to keep up with demand. "Consumer desire for organic, locally-grown strawberries has really ramped up," says Cochran. "Education around organics in the last decade has led to an explosion in demand for our strawberries. The market is expanding faster than our supply."

While demand is up, in the past couple of years yields have been way down. "The culprit is weird weather. Climate change has been bad for business" says Cochran, "No rain and not enough chilling in the winter are the biggest factors." Unseasonably warm winters affect the vigor of the plant. Strawberries thrive with winter chilling. Without it, the plants aren't as robust or big come spring, and supply suffers.

Strawberry picker, Maria Reyes, carries the fruits of her labor.

Still, the farm continues. If Swanton's bustling business at farmers markets—nine stalls around the Bay Area—and busy farmstand traffic are any indication, it is possible to grow luscious fruit, protect the earth, treat workers well, and run a modestly profitable farm at the same time.

Cochran reflects on the raw ingredients a successful farmer needs. "You have to be smart and nimble and very persistent in the face of adversity," he says. "You have to pay close attention to your customers and your employees, and you have to watch your costs. Oh, and you have to be lucky," he adds. "It's tempting to pat yourself on the back after a good year, but a bad year could follow through no fault of your own. But it's an honest living and a good lifestyle if you have the capacity to overcome hurdles and are prepared for the long haul."

Recipes

PANNA COTTA WITH STRAWBERRIES

1 envelope unflavored gelatin
2 tablespoons water
2½ cups whipping cream
½ cup lowfat milk
⅓ cup, plus 2 tablespoons sugar
1½ teaspoons vanilla extract
1 teaspoon orange zest
3 cups strawberries, sliced
juice of ½ lemon

In a small bowl dissolve the gelatin in the water and set aside. In a large saucepan, bring the cream, milk, and ⅓ cup sugar to a boil over medium heat, stirring constantly. Remove from heat and stir in the gelatin mixture, vanilla, and orange zest. Divide between six ½-cup ramekins. Chill covered for four hours or overnight. Before serving, combine strawberries, lemon juice, and 2 tablespoons sugar in a bowl. Mix until the lemon and sugar coat the berries. Spoon over the ramekins of panna cotta and serve.

STRAWBERRY COMPOTE

3 cups fresh strawberries
2 tablespoons sugar
1 tablespoon lemon juice
zest of 1 lemon

Coarsely chop the strawberries and place them in a saucepan. Add the sugar, lemon juice, and lemon zest. Heat the mixture on medium heat, stirring constantly, until the mixture is bubbling, then reduce the heat to low. Continue cooking, stirring occasionally, over low heat for 10 to 12 minutes. Remove from heat and transfer to a clean jar or container to cool thoroughly. Store in the refrigerator.

GOOD LAND ORGANICS

Goleta

· · · · · · · · · · · · · · · · · · ·

IF YOU VISIT:

Info: goodlandorganics.com, 805-685-4189
1362 Farren Road, Goleta

Farm Tours: Three-hour tours, once a month
minimum group size 15 (includes coffee tasting).

Exotics R Us

Call it destiny: farmer Jay Ruskey, the boy who attended Cheremoya Avenue School in Hollywood, grew up to become a leading edible entrepreneur in California's exotic-fruit farming community. And yes, at Ruskey's Good Land Organics, cherimoyas are in the ground, as well as other esoteric offerings such as dragon fruit, finger limes, passion fruit, goji berries, strawberry guava, white sapotes, and yuzu. The cherimoya, a fruit with custard-like flesh, hence its custard-apple nickname, offers a blend of fragrant tropical flavor notes such as coconut, pineapple, mango, papaya, and banana.

Jay Ruskey grows unusual crops.

That's not all: Good Land Organics, situated in the foothills of Santa Barbara just two miles from the coast, is a longtime avocado farm, boasting more than 500 trees of the California native Hass avocado, coveted for its velvety texture and creamy taste. Named after the postal carrier who patented the variety in 1935, these dark-green colored, bumpy-skinned avos are the world's most popular kind.

Wait, there's more. Ruskey lays claim to being the first California grower to plant, harvest, process, and sell coffee on a commercial scale. No joke. For the past dozen years or so, this farmer with a science mind has been experimenting with raising locally grown, organic coffee that's proven a hit with consumers and critics alike. His brew, roasted to order and purchased online, routinely sells out at the Santa Barbara farmers market. And his beans are in high demand internationally—for a premium price. In 2015 he began selling coffee trees as houseplants on the retail market.

Ruskey has long had an interest in growing. He majored in agricultural business and marketing at California Polytechnic State University (Cal Poly) in San Luis Obispo. He harvested flowers for farmers in Carpinteria while in high school.

His degree has come in handy—make no mistake, this risk-taking farmer is a savvy businessman. His 42-acre farm features year-round production, weather willing, which guarantees regular cash flow: cherimoyas are a winter-to-spring crop, avocados ripen from spring through summer, coffee requires most labor from summer to fall, and finger limes are a fall crop.

Adapt and Innovate

Goleta, 10 miles north of Santa Barbara, typically offers a forgiving climate for growers. The farm sits on rich, clay-loam soil. One of Ruskey's biggest challenges? No flat land. Crops are planted on gentle (and not so gentle) slopes, which require careful management during rainy season to ensure proper drainage. The continued drought, of course, has been particularly tough on avocados, resulting in the drastic action known as stumping, or severely cutting back a tree to avoid the need for watering for several months.

"Adapt or die" are words many farmers live by. Ruskey is a fan of innovative ideas to get the best yields from his land while ensuring environmental stewardship. For instance, a visit to the farm reveals passion and dragon fruit vines coexisting with avocado trees. Similarly, coffee plants do well when grown in an established avocado orchard because the crops have similar needs in terms of soil, nutrients, and water. Avocados offer the smaller coffee shrubs protection from winds and shade from the sun. And the

two plants can share an irrigation supply. Rusky calls it layered agriculture.

Dozens of different types of plants, including 1,500 coffee shrubs, five acres of cherimoyas, and three acres of finger limes are grown at Good Land. An Australian native, finger limes are also known as caviar limes for the little juice vesticles or sacs that pop on the tongue. Ruskey tends more than 15 varieties of Arabica type coffee, most commonly Typica and Caturra, which result in high yields and a superior sip.

Ruskey's parents bought the farm back in 1990. He started managing it right away, even though he was still in college. Ruskey became fulltime on the farm in 1996. If it's uncommon, he has probably attempted to grow it. Up next: he's tinkering with black truffles, from the Périgord region of France. These delicacies are prized by chefs and gourmands around the globe for their umami-rich earthy flavor and pungent aroma.

A Buzz for Local Joe

Ruskey is perhaps best known as the coffee guy. Traditionally, coffee is an equatorial crop. But Ruskey teamed up with farm advisor Mark Gaskell of the University of California Division of Agriculture and Natural Resources, Cooperative Extension, to give coffee growing a go in temperate Santa Barbara. Based on his field research in Central America and Hawaii, Gaskell had a hunch that the microclimate there might yield a delicious cup of joe.

Ruskey was willing to gamble on growing the caffeinated crop. He planted his first seeds in 2002. It takes four to five years from seed before a farmer has coffee cherries to harvest, and it was a few years of experimenting before Good Land beans and brews were ready for prime time.

Third Wave coffee fans take note: Santa Barbara java might be the next frontier on the brewing scene. Ruskey is proud of his coffee product: it's so good that no cream or sugar is necessary, he says, because it exhibits the right balance of sweetness, acidity, and body. "It was challenging to begin with. There wasn't a lot of information available about how to grow coffee successfully here, because it hadn't been done before."

"At first we just wanted to see if we could grow a quality crop," says Ruskey, 43, a father of three. "Then we had to learn how to turn that raw ingredient into a processed

bean that results in a really good cup of coffee. Half the work is post harvest."

He began showing up at his local farmers market with some beans back in 2008; by 2010 he had a reliable supply of beans— and more demand than he could meet. But before he found success, he spent a ton of time mastering roasting techniques, which he first attempted on his stovetop with humorous results, says operations manager Lindsey McManus Mesta, who has previous experience growing coffee in Hawaii.

Ruskey is eager to have some local competition to keep things buzzing on the coffee front. He cofounded Diversitree

Nursery to help elevate coffee growing in the region. About a dozen growers in nearby Morro Bay, Mission Canyon, and Carpinteria are also experimenting with coffee crops.

Ruskey foresees a day when the Santa Barbara coast roast is widely available to java junkies near and far, along with other hyper-local blends. He's determined to elevate coffee crops from a novelty produce product to a routine harvest, in the same way that wine grapes, citrus, almonds, and blueberries have all become Golden State staples.

Ruskey's timing is good: consumers are willing to pay for quality caffeine. His coffee

can fetch $60 to $80 a pound on the international market, with much of it being sold in Asia. Locals can scoop up a five-ounce bag for $30. At those prices, it's not a beverage for mass consumption just yet; it's more in the luxury locavore realm.

In 2014 he harvested around 500 pounds of coffee beans; in 2015 he expected to double his production. *Coffee Review* called his coffee a "pungent, deep, sweetly nut-toned" and "exceptional" brew. It was selected by the guide as the No. 27 coffee in its Top 30 Coffees for 2014 and described as "a curiosity from close to home, this first-ever California-grown coffee is impressively balanced, deep, and quietly intricate."

As for Ruskey, he revels in his renegade status. "I love the challenge of getting things that I'm not supposed to be able to grow or sell onto the market. It's the perfect marriage of farming, science, and marketing for me. Where other growers might see obstacles, I see opportunities."

Recipes

FINGER LIME AND NECTARINE SALSA

1 yellow nectarine, coarsely chopped
1 white nectarine, coarsely chopped
⅓ cup red onion, diced
1 red bell pepper, seeded and diced
1 small jalapeño, seeded and minced
½ bunch cilantro, chopped
caviar from two large or three small finger limes
dash of salt

Combine all ingredients in a bowl and stir. Serve with tortilla chips, over grilled fish, or spooned over slices of avocado as a side dish.

CHOCOLATE COVERED COFFEE BEANS

1 cup good quality semi-sweet chocolate
½ cup roasted coffee beans

Coarsely chop the chocolate and then add it to a microwave safe bowl. Warm the chocolate in the microwave at 30 second intervals until the chocolate has melted. Stir the chocolate vigorously with a spoon until it's uniform and slightly shiny. Pour the roasted coffee beans into the bowl of melted chocolate and stir until the coffee beans are thoroughly coated with chocolate.

Using a fork, remove the beans, one at a time, or in small clumps and place them on a parchment covered pan to cool.
Allow to cool completely.

HILLTOP & CANYON FARMS

Carpinteria

. . . .

IF YOU VISIT:

Location: 6754 Rincon Road, Carpinteria

Farmstand: Not on site

Find the farmers: At local farmers markets including Tuesday and Saturday in downtown Santa Barbara, Friday in Montecito, and Sunday in Ojai.

Farmers Market Enthusiasts

Tessa van der Werff brings her baby to work, which means wearing her in a front carrier while she goes about the business of weeding. She also cuts a colorful collection of field flowers such as cosmos, bachelor's buttons, larkspur, zinnias, and sunflowers, for that day's farmers market with her baby on board. The farmer grows 30 different types of eye-catching and fragrant field flowers, which she arranges into mixed bouquets.

It's a family owned and operated business. She and her husband Robert Abbott run Hilltop & Canyon Farms, an organic operation that specializes in citrus, avocados, flower bouquets, heirloom beans, and assorted other specialty crops. Abbott's family has been farming the land in this Southern California coastal town since 1923 when his grandfather bought the property. Abbott's father was an early pioneer in the emerging local avocado industry. Much of the lower farm is still planted with avocados—some of the trees date back seven decades and remain strong producers.

The pair creates popular products from raw farm materials. They're known locally for their wooden cutting boards, handcrafted from milled olive tree wood, sourced on site. They also preserve produce. Eureka and Lisbon lemons end up bottled in a salty brine. Preserved lemons are a popular addition to pastas and tagines and are used in marinades and salad dressings. Mild, smoky shishito peppers, which originate from Japan, get pickled, too, and mixed with orange zest and spices, like coriander and fennel seed.

The couple farm 10 acres of the 12-acre property. Like a lot of small-scale farmers, they're big farmers market boosters. Working the land can be a tough a way to make a living, and it can feel isolating. Along with striving to grow quality crops, there's the fickleness of the wholesale market, and the unpredictability of the weather—hello climate change and drought. For the past decade or so, however, farmers markets have proved a constant, stable source of income and connection. "Nothing beats showing up at the farmers market with a truckload of the best stuff we can grow and getting it into the hands of our enthusiastic and supportive customers, many of whom are regulars," says Abbott. "It's a win-win: Our customers get to go home and enjoy good food that will sustain them, and we're able to make a living from our labor."

Tessa van der Werff is raising her family in the fields.

The wholesale market is another matter. Price fluctuations for produce like avocados and lemons are common; a glut of produce means prices plummet downward. For every good earning year there's often a string of years where the farm barely breaks even. Still, the Abbott clan has endured. The family has been growing the same crop for close to a century, a pretty impressive track record. Abbott has faith that he'll continue to make an income from producing food in what he calls one of the world's greatest growing regions for subtropical fruit like avocados and citrus.

In addition to his role in the community as a farmer, Abbott sees himself as an educator. American food culture, he says, is still in its infancy. It's hard to believe, but it's true: There are people who don't know what an avocado is. People have asked Abbott whether they should boil or bake the creamy fruit. Another reason why he loves the farmers market route: One-on-one, on-the-spot education. Though with three children under the age of 7, he's at the markets less often than when he and van der Werff began farming together in 2005. These days, a farmstand manager sells the family's bounty.

Working With Nature

Abbott says despite all the hurdles that today's sustainable farmers face—including water and land costs, pressure from pests and domestic and international competition—he's optimistic about the future. "We farm because we believe people should know where their food comes from, who grew it, and the best ways to eat it," he says. "We also farm because it builds community, helps the local economy, feeds our family, and it's creative: there's something new to discover every day."

More than anything, Abbott farms because he has to. "I live for early mornings when the plants—and my back—are fresh. We both enjoy the manual labor and we aren't afraid of physical work. At the end of the day, we have tangible proof of what we can do as a team and that's incredibly satisfying."

A committed environmental steward active in local watershed restoration, Abbott transitioned the third-generation farm to organic methods more than a dozen years ago. He favors an "if you can't beat 'em, join 'em" approach to dealing with weeds and pests. With perseverance and an open

Good Land Organics

CeRTified OrgANIC

AVOCADOS
'HASS'

$3⁵⁰ per lb

GROWN IN CARPINTERIA!

mind when it comes to trying different strategies, such as homegrown compost, mulch, and cover cropping, the farm has endured. "I'd much rather work with nature than against it," says Abbott. "It's as simple as that."

The couple, in their late 30s, are raising three daughters on the farm: Edie, 7, Bea, 4, and Zinnia, 1. The children have spent a lot of time with their parents on the property. "They hang out with us here. My oldest, Edie, likes to help pick flowers and arrange bouquets; they're happy to spend time in the fields," says van der Werff. "They come up with creative stuff to do."

Van der Werff, who had no previous farming background, met Abbott when she was working in outdoor education at the Chewonki Semester School in Wiscasset, Maine. Abbott was working at the school's summer camp. After they became an item, Tessa agreed to move back to the family farm. For four years she worked at The Center for Urban Agriculture at Fairview Gardens, a nonprofit farm in nearby Goleta, before the pair decided to make the leap to working together. Unlike some long-term farmer/owners, this couple, who has five employees, can be found in the fields on a regular basis weeding, watering, and harvesting.

The Power of Two

Over the years, they say, they found their rhythm together and have settled into a comfortable partnership. They divide and conquer: He tends to do the tractor work; she's partial to seed selection and handpicking. Abbott does most of the care and feeding of the chicken coop, home to more than 160 hens. They complement each other in other ways.

"I'm the gas pedal, and she's the brakes," says Abbott.

"Robert wants to do everything—at once—and sometimes we get a little tired," jokes his other half. "So I'm the voice of reason: We really can't do it all. Having young children certainly makes us evaluate what is realistic."

Sometimes it's necessary to pivot, take stock, and adjust. On any farm, there is always more work to be done.

This husband-and-wife team expects to continue the family legacy, and perhaps pass it on. "I hope the farm stays in the family, that the girls inherit a love for the land that Tessa and I both share," says Abbott. "Who knows, maybe when they're teenagers they'll want to take off for New York City. But I would love to see the fourth-generation of Abbotts continue this work. The land has been good to us. It can be good to the next generation, too."

Recipes

QUICK PRESERVED LEMONS

6 lemons, scrubbed, ends trimmed, and cut lengthwise into six wedges

3 tablespoons coarse sea salt

approximately 2 cups fresh lemon juice (enough to cover the lemons once placed in the pan)

Preheat the oven to 200 degrees F. Place lemon wedges in a baking dish (just large enough to hold the lemons in one layer) and toss them with the sea salt. Pour lemon juice over the salted wedges until they are just covered. Cover the pan with tin foil and bake, stirring occasionally, for 3 hours. Let the lemons cool and transfer them, and the pan juice, into a sterilized jar and refrigerate until used.

ROASTED CITRUS AND AVOCADO SALAD

1 lemon, sliced into ⅛-inch rounds, with seeds removed

1 small orange, sliced into ⅛-inch rounds, with seeds removed

1 tablespoon, organic coconut oil, melted

2 tablespoons sugar

1 head young red leaf lettuce, cleaned and torn into bite-size pieces

¼ cup thinly sliced red onion

¼ cup fresh cilantro, coarsely chopped

1 avocado, sliced into ¼-inch wedges

salad dressing:

¼ cup olive oil

2 tablespoons fresh lemon juice

pinch of coarse sea salt

Preheat oven to 425 degrees F. Toss lemon slices, orange slices, melted coconut oil, and sugar in a bowl until evenly coated. Transfer the lemon and orange slices onto a rimmed baking sheet and bake (turning after 7 minutes) until the rind and pulp are lightly browned, 12 to 15 minutes. Remove from the pan immediately and let cool.

Combine salad dressing ingredients in a small bowl and whisk until creamy.

Place the cooled lemons and oranges in a bowl with lettuce, onion, chopped cilantro, and avocado wedges. Drizzle on the salad dressing and gently toss to coat, being careful not to mash the avocado.

Acknowledgments

So many good people played a role in making this book a reality. Allow me to give a shout out to them here.

Up first: my partner on *Farmsteads,* the uber-talented photographer Erin Scott. Erin recommended me for this project. She thought it was solidly in my wheelhouse. She was right. Erin was a delight to work with: she gets as excited as I do about spending a day in dirt. Her creativity, masterful visual storytelling, and astute eye for detail are apparent in every page of this book. Also, it must be said: she did most of the driving in her non-crappy car, and proved an ideal companion on the road. We witnessed meteors in the sky in the way-too-early hours of the morning, endured unseasonably scorching days in the fields, and got jazzed by the same people and places. I am grateful that we were on the same page about how this book would look: I completely trusted that she would deliver on the photography front. And I think readers will agree she did so to glorious effect.

This book would not have happened without the enthusiasm of publisher Lisa McGuinness. *Farmsteads* was her idea, born out of a visit to Harley Farms Goat Dairy, which inspired Lisa to want to know more about the coastal farmers who grow our food. Thank you, Lisa, for taking a chance on me, being generous with your vision, and open to ideas. Constant companions throughout this project: Lisa's kindness, humor, and patience.

Thanks, as well, to Rose Wright for her clean and crisp design and for barbecuing oysters on a workday by the bay. Hat tips to copyeditor Kim Carpenter and proofreader Amy Bauman for their keen eyes for stray or absent commas and such. And a big thanks to my longtime colleague and friend, editor Diana Hembree, who read every word and weighed in with timely tweaks.

Much gratitude to Alice Waters, Novella Carpenter, Naomi Starkman, Cheryl Sternman Rule, and Gibson Thomas for their generous and thoughtful commentary on these pages.

The Mesa Refuge in Point Reyes—one of my favorite places in the world—selected me for a 2015 writing residency. Drafts of the profiles here were written at this West Marin sanctuary for authors. I am so grateful: I couldn't have asked for a more perfect place to craft this book.

Thanks, too, to editors at outlets such as Civil Eats, Modern Farmer, *Edible Marin & Wine Country, Edible San Francisco*, and *Edible East Bay*, for featuring my farm and food stories over the past five years.

To all my galpals—you know who you are, too many of you to name individually—who cheered me on during the writing of this book, thank you for your encouragement and support. Thanks as well to my family back home and my Aussie posse, who have always believed I had a book in me.

This book is for Gabe, my number one son, who shares my hunger for farm-fresh produce like no other teenager I know. I am lucky my boy is curious about all things culinary, and appreciates a lovely meal along with a good belly laugh. Feeding him is one of my greatest joys.

Finally, *Farmsteads* is dedicated to the dozen farmers featured in these pages. Thank you for your hard work, feeding us well, caring about the natural environment, protecting precious resources, and sharing your stories.

Sarah Henry is a seasoned eater, reader, and writer. Her farm and food stories have appeared in print in a wide range of publications, including *AFAR*, the *Washington Post*, the *San Francisco Chronicle, California*, and *Cherry Bombe*, and online at Civil Eats, CHOW, KQED, Lucky Peach, and Modern Farmer.

She is a regular contributor to *Edible San Francisco, Edible East Bay*, and *Edible Marin & Wine Country*. Find her in *Best Food Writing 2014, Best Food Writing 2015*, and at sarahhenrywriter.com. Henry lives in the Bay Area, where she's a wannabe urban farmer. Her Twitter handle is, of course, @lettuceeatkale.

Erin Scott is a food and lifestyle photographer, and author of the *Yummy Supper* cookbook. Raised by parents who were avid vegetable gardeners, environmentalists, and organic farming advocates, Scott's appreciation for farmers and their bounty runs deep. She lives with her husband and two kids in Berkeley, California, where she spends her free time cooking, eating, and photographing whatever sprouts in her backyard veggie patch.

Scott's work has been featured in *Kinfolk*, the *San Francisco Chronicle, Saveur, Edible Marin & Wine Country*, Jamie Oliver's Food Revolution, The Huffington Post, *7x7*, Design Sponge, *Mother Earth Living*, and Food52.